W9-AON-172

Lively Bible Lessons for Grades K-3

Loveland, Colorado

Lively Bible Lessons for Grades K-3
Copyright © 1991 by Group Publishing, Inc.

All rights reserved. No part of this book may be reproduced in any manner whatsoever without prior written permission from the publisher, except where noted in the text and in the case of brief quotations embodied in critical articles and reviews. For information write Permissions, Group Publishing, Inc., Dept. BK, Box 481, Loveland, CO 80539.

Credits
Edited by Cindy S. Hansen
Cover and interior designed by Jill Christopher
Illustrations by Jan Knudson

Unless otherwise noted, scriptures quoted from **The Everyday Bible, New Century Version**, copyright © 1987, 1988 by Word Publishing, Dallas, Texas 75039. Used by permission.

Library of Congress Cataloging-in-Publication Data

ISBN 1-55945-074-6
14 13 12 11 10 9 8 7 6 03 02 01 00 99 98 97 96
Printed in the United States of America.

CONTENTS

Part 3: A Lively Look at My Faith

Part 4: A Lively Look at Celebrations

INTRODUCTION

Welcome to a resource filled with lively, active Bible lessons for children in kindergarten through the third grade. Here are fun meetings that'll hold your kids' attention and teach self-esteem-building, friendship-boosting, faith-developing topics.

In *Lively Bible Lessons for Grades K-3*, Sunday school teachers, vacation Bible school teachers, after-school program directors and any leader of young children will find 20 simple-to-follow lessons that combine lively learning, colorful art projects and scrumptious snacks.

The book is divided into these four parts:

● **Part 1: A Lively Look at Myself**—Children are growing and changing daily. This section covers topics that help kids with security, worries, fears and self-esteem.

● **Part 2: A Lively Look at My Relationships**—This section helps children look past themselves to others. Topics include helping others, problem-solving, peer groups, friendship and acceptance.

● **Part 3: A Lively Look at My Faith**—Children are interested in God, the church and their developing faith. Faith-building topics include heaven, sin, forgiveness, and more about God and his son, Jesus.

● **Part 4: A Lively Look at Celebrations**—People of all ages love to celebrate special occasions. This section offers Bible lessons and celebrations for birthdays, Easter, Thanksgiving and Christmas.

THE LIVELY BIBLE LESSONS

The lessons in *Lively Bible Lessons for Grades K-3* each contain at least seven activities. Each activity lasts no longer than eight minutes. The activities are fast-paced for children with short attention spans. Each lesson is divided into the following elements:

● **Introduction**—One or two paragraphs that give an overview of the lesson's topic.

● **A Powerful Purpose**—A short statement of the lesson's objective, telling what children will learn.

● **A Look at the Lesson**—An outline including activity titles and estimated completion time. These times may vary depending on your class size.

● **A Sprinkling of Supplies**—A list of all items you'll need for the lesson.

● **The Lively Lesson**—Quick, active, reflective, scripture-based activities. Lessons start with an opening experience to set the mood for the upcoming lesson. Kids experience the topics through active learning using their senses of hearing, seeing, smelling, tasting and feeling.

Lessons include participation Bible stories, action-packed memory verses, action songs to familiar tunes, art projects and snacks.

● **Handouts**—All necessary handouts are included. They're easy to use and you have permission to photocopy them for local church use.

Enjoy *Lively Bible Lessons for Grades K-3*. Use and adapt the Bible lessons for any gathering of children. Watch kids develop self-esteem, meet new friends and grow in their faith. And have fun teaching topics in an active, lively and meaningful way!

Part 1: A Lively Look at Myself

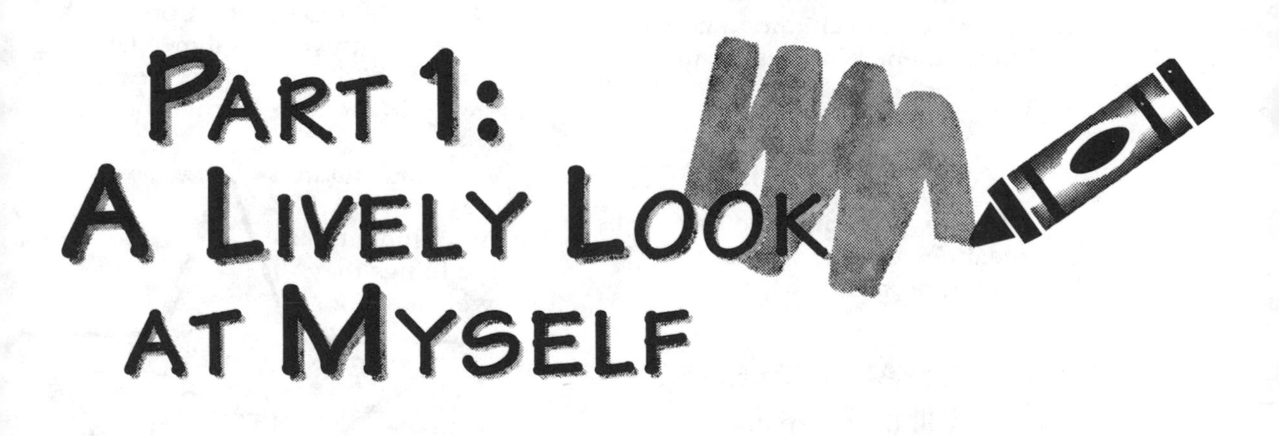

STRENGTH BOMBARDMENT

Primary children are beginning to notice their own strengths and weaknesses. They're concerned about things they don't do well—especially if they have friends who seem to be perfect. And it's often hard for children to affirm their own strengths.

Helping children accept themselves—including their strengths and weaknesses—is important. Use this lesson to help children know that God loves them regardless of their successes or failures.

A POWERFUL PURPOSE

Children will identify their strengths and weaknesses. They'll hear that God loves them no matter what.

A LOOK AT THE LESSON

1. Do-Well Boards (6 minutes)
2. Do-Well Parade (7 minutes)
3. Superstar Strength Bombardment (5 minutes)
4. We're Human (5 minutes)
5. Hip, Hip, Hurray (6 minutes)
6. Strength Food (6 minutes)
7. Time to Pray (6 minutes)

A SPRINKLING OF SUPPLIES

Gather a Bible, posterboard, crayons, scissors, yarn, a hole punch, balloons, markers, napkins, apples and oranges. For each person, you'll need a sheet of self-sticking stars.

THE LIVELY LESSON

1. Do-Well Boards

(You'll need crayons, yarn, a hole punch, scissors and a piece of posterboard for each child. For each young person, make a do-well board as shown in the "Sandwich Board" diagram. Cut a piece of posterboard in half. Lay the sides together and punch a hole in each top corner. Connect the two halves with yarn so they'll lay across the child's shoulders, creating a sandwich board sign on the front and back.)

Welcome children as they arrive. Ask them to think about all the things they do well at school, such as math or spelling; at home, such as riding a bike or playing the piano; at church, such as helping a teacher or singing in the choir; and with friends, such as helping a friend wash his or her dog. Tell them they're going to have a chance to tell others about their accomplishments.

SANDWICH BOARD

Show them the do-well boards you made out of yarn and posterboard.

Demonstrate how one fits over your shoulders. Explain that they're really called sandwich boards. Some store owners hire people to slip the sandwich board over their head and walk in front of their business. Advertising for the business is written on the board. They will "advertise" what they do well the same way.

Hand out the crayons. Have the kids each design the front and back of their board using words or pictures of things they do well. When they finish they can help others with their boards.

2. Do-Well Parade

(If possible, arrange for children to walk in a parade through other classes that are being held at the same time. If that's not possible, simply hold the parade in your room. You'll need a Bible.)

When children finish their do-well boards, have them stand in a straight line. Teach this song to the tune of "Three Blind Mice."

This is me. This is me.
What I do well. What I do well.
Let me shout out what I do well.
Let me shout out what I do well.
Hip, hip, hurray. Hip, hip, hurray.

Once they memorize the song, say: **We're going to walk in a do-well parade. Let's march around the room and sing our song.**

Gather in a circle and ask children to tell about some of the items on their do-well boards. Ask:

● **Was it easy deciding what you do well? Why?**

● **Why is it important to feel good about the things you do well?**

● **Why does God want you to be happy about what you do well?**

● **What could you do if you had a friend who thought he or she couldn't do anything well?**

Say: **God wants us to do our best with our abilities. He also wants us to make other people feel good about themselves. Some of us can run fast and some of us can't. But we are still important. Some of us are good at math, and some are good at spelling. God gave every person things he or she can do well. Here's how important we are to God.**

Read Psalm 8:3-6 from a children's Bible, or use this version: **"I look at your heavens, which you made with your fingers. I see the moon and stars, which you created. But why are people important to you? Why do you take care of human beings? You made them a little lower than the angels and crowned them with glory and honor. You put them in charge of everything you made. You put all things under their control."**

3. Superstar Strength Bombardment

(You'll need a sheet of self-sticking stars for each person. Each sheet should contain a number of stars equal to the number of participants. Using one chair for each person, set chairs in a circle.

Ask the children to take off their do-well boards, then sit in the chairs that are arranged in a circle. You stand in the center. Say: **Look around the circle at one another. Think about what you like about each person. For example, you may like someone because he laughs at your jokes. Or, you may like someone because she says nice things to you. I'm going to give you a sheet**

of stars. (Hand them out.) **Each one of you will take a turn standing in the center. One at a time the others will come up to you and say, "I like you because you . . ." and then they'll stick a star on your arm. Let's begin with the oldest person.**

Make sure each person gets to be a superstar in the center chair. Start off each child's affirmation yourself, so the others see how to do it.

Afterward say: **Look at all the stars stuck on you. They show you're a special person. A superstar. Each of those stars is something we like about you.** Ask:

- **How do you feel right now?**
- **How did you feel telling others things you liked about them?**

Say: **God wants us to help others feel good. We do that when we tell them things we like about them.**

Let kids put the stars from their arms on their do-well boards.

4. We're Human

(You'll need an inflated balloon and a marker for each child.)

Say: **This next activity is harder, but I know you can do it. We just celebrated good things about ourselves. But we sometimes do things we don't like. We get angry, frustrated, and do mean things.** Give children each an inflated balloon and a marker. Ask the kids to draw on the balloon something they'd like to improve about themselves. For example, if they want to improve their temper they could draw a mad face.

Place the balloons on the floor, then gather in a circle around them. Ask kids to take off their shoes. Say: **Let's all "stomp out" these things by stomping on the balloons.**

When the balloons are popped, ask the children to put the shriveled balloons in a pile. Say: **God believes in our strengths more than our weaknesses. God also wants us to tell him about our troubles. Jesus said to ask and we will receive. When we feel down, we should talk to God. He'll help pick us up.**

5. Hip, Hip, Hurray

(You'll need the do-well boards.)

Ask kids to put on their do-well boards. Have them each look at the boards and decide on one thing they do best. When you point to each child, he or she should say, "I am good at . . ." and complete the sentence with something he or she does well. Afterward the group will shout, "Hip, hip, hurray for you."

Do this for each person randomly around the room.

6. Strength Food

(You'll need napkins, and apples and oranges prepared to serve.)

Serve the apples and oranges as a snack. Talk about how fruit helps us grow strong and stay healthy. As you munch on the oranges, take turns completing this sentence, "Orange you glad you can . . .?" For example, "Orange you glad you can run fast?" "Orange you glad you can come to church to worship God?"

7. Time to Pray

Remind children to take home their do-well boards and hang them in their rooms. When they see the stars on the boards they can remember all the good things people said about them.

Close by asking God to help kids appreciate what they do well.

by Mike Gillespie

Those Worries and Fears

Children are vulnerable to worry and fear. The fear of losing a parent, the fear of being alone in the dark. Worries about a best friend moving away or a new school year beginning.

Use this lesson to help kids talk about their fears and worries and see that God is there through these tough times.

A POWERFUL PURPOSE

Children will identify their worries and fears and know that God can help overcome them.

A LOOK AT THE LESSON

1. Worry Wagon (8 minutes)
2. Trapped by Our Worries and Fears (4 minutes)
3. Advice From Paul and Jesus (6 minutes)
4. Worry and Fear Giveaway (8 minutes)
5. Lesson From Jonah (8 minutes)
6. Psalm Power (5 minutes)
7. Eat Your Worries and Fears (6 minutes)

A SPRINKLING OF SUPPLIES

Gather a Bible, a small wagon, construction paper, newsprint, a marker, crayons, a box, bread and squeeze bottles of honey. You'll also need a photocopy of the "Psalm Power" handout for each child.

THE LIVELY LESSON

1. Worry Wagon

(Cut flag shapes and wagon shapes out of construction paper as shown in the "Flags and Wagons" diagram. Make at least two flags and two wagons per child. On another piece of construction paper, write "Worry Wagon" and tape it to a children's toy wagon.)

Welcome children as they arrive. Give them each two paper wagon shapes, two paper flag shapes and crayons.

FLAGS AND WAGONS

Pull the Worry Wagon in front of the kids, and explain that they're going to talk about worries and fears.

Hold up a flag shape and say: **This is a fear flag. Think of one or two things you're afraid of like being in the dark or being left alone. Draw each fear on a fear flag.** Show kids that for fear of the dark they could color the flag black. For fear of being alone they could draw one face on a flag.

Hold up a wagon shape and say: **This is a worry wagon. Think of one or two worries like having a**

new teacher or not doing well in school. Draw each worry on a worry wagon. Show children they could draw a stick figure to represent worry about a new teacher, or they could draw a big red X through the wagon to show worry about not doing well in school.

Allow time for students to draw. Then invite them to put their fear flags and worry wagons inside the big Worry Wagon.

2. Trapped by Our Worries and Fears

(You'll need a marker and the Worry Wagon. Tape newsprint to the wall.)

Gather in a circle. Ask a child to pull the Worry Wagon around the outside of the group several times. Say: **Well, let's pretend we are being circled by our worries and fears. They're very powerful. We're trapped by them. Let's find out about them.**

Instruct the wagon puller to stop at each child and have him or her pull out a flag or wagon shape. Let each child try to figure out what fear or worry the drawing depicts. Ask kids to name the worries or fears as you write them on the newsprint.

Say: **That's quite a list. I wonder if the Bible can help us with our worries and fears. Let's take a look.**

3. Advice From Paul and Jesus

(You'll need a Bible.)

Tell the kids that Jesus spent a day with lots of people listening to him. He talked a long time. One of the things he talked about that day had to do with worry.

Read Matthew 6:25-26 from a children's Bible, or read this version: **"So I tell you, don't worry about the food you need to live. And don't worry about the clothes you need for your body. Life is more important than food. And the body is more important than clothes. Look at the birds in the air. They don't plant or harvest or store food in barns. But your heavenly Father feeds the birds. And you know that you are worth much more than the birds."**

Ask kids why they think Jesus told us not to worry about those things. Say: **Jesus wanted us to trust God. God loves us so much that he takes care of us. God helps us get over our worries and fears.**

Have the kids stand and chant three times, "Don't worry. Trust God."

Tell the children that the apostle Paul wrote a letter to the church at a place called Philippi. Read Philippians 4:6: **"Do not worry about anything. But pray and ask God for everything you need. And when you pray, always give thanks."**

Say: **Paul told the people to turn their worries over to God. The same advice Jesus gave us.**

Have the kids stand and chant three times, "Don't worry. Trust God."

4. Worry and Fear Giveaway

(You'll need a box, a marker, and the wagon filled with fears and worries. Arrange to take your class into the worship area briefly during this activity.)

Address the box, "To God in Heaven." Read the words as you address the box. Ask the kids to help you place all the paper fear flags and worry wagons inside the box.

Lead the group into your worship

area and place the box on the altar. Pray together sending all those worries and fears off to God. Leave the box on the altar and return to your meeting area.

5. Lesson From Jonah

Say: **The Bible tells about a man named Jonah. We can learn a lot about our worries and fears by hearing the story.** Tell the following story of Jonah and ask the kids to imitate whatever you do.

There was once a man that God wanted for a special job. (Point to yourself proudly.)

When God told Jonah what he wanted him to do, Jonah didn't like it. He decided to run away from God. (Run in place.)

Jonah jumped on a ship to escape from God. (Jump up and down.)

While the ship was at sea, a terrible storm came. (Blow in the air and rock back and forth.)

Men on the boat asked Jonah why he was on board. Jonah told them he was running away from God and that God was mad at him. (Run in place.)

The men decided that Jonah was causing the storm so they threw him into the sea. (Pretend to dive.)

The storm stopped and the sea got calm. (Do a "shhh ...")

Suddenly a giant fish came and swallowed Jonah. (Do a gulping action three times.)

Jonah was scared. He was lonely. There was no one to help him. (Pretend to bite nails like you're scared.)

Jonah decided to pray for help. He asked God to save him from the fish. (Fold hands as in prayer.)

God heard Jonah's prayer, and the fish spit him out on the shore. Jonah was saved. (Jump up and down like you're celebrating.)

Jonah went to the evil city of Nineveh and told the people to repent. (Shake your finger like you're scolding.)

They did. (Clap with joy.)

Say: **Jonah got himself in a big mess. But when he prayed, God heard his prayer. Sometimes you may be afraid or worried and think no one can help. But God can. God is always there.**

6. Psalm Power

(You'll need photocopies of the "Psalm Power" handout and crayons.)

Pass out the "Psalm Power" handouts and crayons. Read the psalm to the kids. Ask them to color the sheet. When they finish, say: **The Lord is my light and the one who saves me.** The kids say: "I fear no one." You say: **The Lord protects my life.** Have the kids say: "I am afraid of no one." Repeat this three times.

Tell the kids to hang this Psalm in their rooms as a reminder of God's help when they're afraid.

7. Eat Your Worries and Fears

(You'll need bread and squeeze bottles of honey for kids to share.)

Give children each some honey in a squeeze bottle and a piece of bread. Ask them each to draw a sad, worried face on the piece of bread with the honey.

After they draw their sad, worried faces, tell them to eat the bread as a symbol of turning worry or fear over to God. It's gone!

by Mike Gillespie

Permission to photocopy this handout granted for local church use. Copyright © Group Books, Box 481, Loveland, CO 80539.

Anger Cure: Forgiveness

It's never easy to forgive someone, no matter how old you are. Primary children are being inundated with new experiences, and they're just beginning to maneuver the tricky waters of relationships.

Use this lesson to help children see how anger can hurt them and hold them back from really enjoying each other. Let kids know that forgiving feels good and is what God wants from them.

A POWERFUL PURPOSE

Children will learn to overcome anger and forgive others.

A LOOK AT THE LESSON

1. Bucket Race (8 minutes)
2. Weighed Down (4 minutes)
3. Tangled Up (8 minutes)
4. Anger Cure: Forgiveness (6 minutes)
5. Licorice Knots (8 minutes)
6. Making the Knots Disappear (4 minutes)
7. Forgiveness Prayer (2 minutes)

A SPRINKLING OF SUPPLIES

Gather a Bible, two buckets of sand (or two heavy books), two chairs, a ball of red yarn, photocopies of the "Anger Cure: Forgiveness" handout, crayons and licorice strings.

THE LIVELY LESSON

1. Bucket Race

(You'll need two buckets of sand or two heavy books—heavy enough so kids will have some difficulty carrying them but not so heavy that they strain their muscles. Place two chairs at one side of the room.)

Form two teams. Ask the teams to line up on the side of the room opposite the two chairs.

Give each team a bucket of sand. Explain that team members must, one at a time, carry the bucket across the room, around the chair, back to their team, and pass it to the next person. All team members must carry the bucket. First team done wins.

Run the race a second time, this time without using the buckets.

2. Weighed Down

Gather kids in a circle and let them catch their breath from the relays. Ask: **Which race was easier to run? Why?**

Say: **It isn't easy to do things when you're carrying something heavy, is it? The weight kept you from doing your best. Did you know that we all have something that can keep us from doing our best for others and for God? That something is anger.**

Ask:

- **How many of you have ever been mad at someone?**

● **What makes you mad?**

● **How did it feel to be angry? Did it feel good?**

3. Tangled Up

(You'll need a ball of red yarn.)

Bring out a large ball of yarn. Have kids stand up in the circle. Ask one child to hold on to the loose end of the yarn ball, then toss the yarn ball to another child while still holding the end. That child catches the ball, takes hold of the yarn, then tosses the ball to someone else. Keep going until all kids are holding a piece of the tangled web of yarn.

Say: **A saying is that "we see red" when we're angry. Look at this red tangled web of yarn and think of times you've been mad, or tangled up in anger. What makes you mad?** Go around the circle and let each person say one thing that makes him or her mad.

4. Anger Cure: Forgiveness

(You'll need photocopies of the "Anger Cure: Forgiveness" handouts and crayons.)

Have kids keep holding the tangled web of yarn. Ask: **Who knows what forgiveness is?**

Say: **Forgiveness gets rid of the tangled feelings of anger. Forgiveness wipes out the anger bug.**

Have kids each think of one person who's done something bad to them lately. Then, one at a time, have them each think about that person and say "I forgive you" as they drop their part of the yarn.

Hand out the "Anger Cure: Forgiveness" handouts and crayons. Read the following Bible verses about forgiveness while kids are decorating their handouts.

● **"Forgive other people, and you will be forgiven" (Luke 6:37).**

● **"Do not be angry with each other, but forgive each other. If someone does wrong to you, then forgive him. Forgive each other because the Lord forgave you" (Colossians 3:13).**

● **"Your sins are forgiven through Christ" (1 John 2:12).**

5. Licorice Knots

(You'll need two strings of licorice for each person.)

Tell children you're going to read some situations. Have them each tie a knot in their licorice if the situation makes them mad. If they can't tie a knot yet, they can twist the licorice.

● **You and your friend Billy are playing tag. Billy gets rougher the longer you play. You've asked him to be nice, but he doesn't listen. Finally, he tags you so hard you fall down and hurt your knee. If this situation would make you mad, knot or twist your licorice.**

● **You are in the recess line at school, waiting to go inside. Carol cuts in front of you in line, elbowing you out of the way. If this situation would make you mad, knot or twist your licorice.**

● **Your brother wants you to play with him, but you're busy. He lies to your mom, saying you hit him. She makes you go to your room. If this situation would make you mad, knot or twist your licorice.**

Say: **Look at your twisted and knotted licorice. That's what anger makes us feel like: twisted up inside. How could we untangle the hurt feelings in these situations?**

Permission to photocopy this handout granted for local church use. Copyright © Group Books, Box 481, Loveland, CO 80539.

6. Making the Knots Disappear

(You'll need the knotted licorice and some extra.)

Have kids listen to some more situations, having them each eat a piece of their licorice if the situation would make them feel better.

- **Billy is sorry he pushed you so hard when you were playing tag. He helps you up and says he's sorry. You forgive him. If the forgiveness makes you feel better, eat a bite of your knotted licorice.**
- **You're lining up to be dismissed from class. Carol cuts in front of you again. You tell her to go to the end of the line. She does. You forgive her. If the forgiveness makes you feel better, eat a bite of your knotted licorice.**
- **Your brother feels bad about lying to your mom. He tells the truth and apologizes to you and your mother. Both you and your mother forgive your brother. If the forgiveness makes the situation feel better, eat a bite of your knotted licorice.**

Say: **In cases where we used to be angry, forgiveness can make us feel better.**

Pass out more licorice and continue the snack time.

7. Forgiveness Prayer

Join hands in an untangled circle. Pray: **God, help us when we're tangled up in anger. Untangle our anger with forgiveness. Thank you for loving us enough to forgive us. Help us forgive others too. Help us know when we should ask people to forgive us. Amen.**

Let children take home their handouts as a reminder to enjoy forgiveness.

by Karen M. Ball

God Takes Care of Us

The world can overwhelm children. They reach out to grasp a parent's hand, hanging on for security in that firm but gentle grip. Children need reassurance that they're safe, that all is well in the world, and that someone bigger and stronger is in control.

Use this lesson to help children learn that Someone even bigger and stronger than a parent is watching out and taking care of them.

A Powerful Purpose

Children will learn that God is their security.

A Look at the Lesson

1. Balancing Act (8 minutes)
2. Going on a Lion Hunt (5 minutes)
3. The Lions' Den (6 minutes)
4. Eatin' Meetin' (5 minutes)
5. Rock Painting (8 minutes)
6. Beach Ball Toss (8 minutes)
7. We're in God's Hands (5 minutes)

A Sprinkling of Supplies

Gather a flashlight, a Bible, animal crackers, tempera paints, paintbrushes, newspapers, old shirts or aprons, mats, two footstools, a beach ball, and a 6-foot long 2×4 to use as a balance beam. You'll also need a small rock for each person.

The Lively Lesson

1. Balancing Act

(Place some mats on the floor. Or, if the weather is nice, do this activity on the grass outside. You'll need the 6-foot long 2×4. Lay it on the mats. You'll also need two footstools.)

Gather kids around the 6-foot piece of wood on the floor. Let them take turns walking the length of it—like a balance beam.

Next, raise the balance beam a couple of feet by placing each end on a footstool. Now ask for volunteers. After they hesitate, say you'll hold their hand as they walk across.

Have one person at a time walk across the beam while the others sit and watch. Give children each a chance to cross the beam. Be sure they don't fall.

Talk about how balancing on the beam was scary, but they felt better holding onto your hand as they crossed. Say: **Jesus can make you feel secure too. He's always by your side with his hand reaching out to keep you safe and secure.**

2. Going on a Lion Hunt

Tell kids you want to lead them in a rhythmic chant to prepare them for the Bible study about Daniel in the lions' den. Have kids make a marching sound by patting their knees with their hands. One, two, one, two; keep the rhythm going as they repeat each line after you.

Going on a lion hunt.
I'm not afraid.
Got my God
And a Bible by my side.

Going on a lion hunt.
Listen to the roar.
See the teeth
And the big, sharp claws.

All those things can't hurt me.
So I'm not afraid.
With my God
And a Bible by my side.

3. The Lions' Den

(Bring a flashlight and a Bible. Use an empty, dark room or a storage closet as the lions' den.)

Say: **We're going on our lion hunt now. Follow me to the lions' home, which is called a den.** Have kids follow you to a storage closet or a small room with the lights out.

Turn on your flashlight and bring out your Bible. Welcome kids to the lions' den. Ask them to get comfortable and listen as you read about Daniel in the lions' den found in Daniel 6:1-23.

Say: **Daniel had a lot to be afraid of, but God kept him safe.** Ask:

- **What are some things you're afraid of?**
- **How do you get over your fear?**

4. Eatin' Meetin'

(You'll need some sort of animal snack, such as animal crackers or Teddy Grahams.)

March back from the lions' den to your meeting room. Gather in a circle and serve your animal snack. Say: **Eat the animal snacks. They can't hurt you. In the Bible, when God's angels were protecting Daniel, he was in no more danger than you are now. Since God was in control, Daniel was safe.**

5. Rock Painting

(You'll need rocks, paints, paintbrushes, and old shirts or aprons. Cover the painting area with newspapers.)

Say: **The Bible tells us to trust God always. He's our security. He's our rock. He takes care of us when we're afraid. As the Bible says in Psalm 18:2: "The Lord is my rock, my protection, my Savior. My God is my rock. I can run to him for safety."**

We're going to paint a rock to remind us that God is solid and strong like a rock. We can depend on him.

Cover kids' good clothes with old shirts or aprons. Supply paints, brushes and rocks. Let their creativity go. They can design the rocks with circles, stripes, crosses, anything to remind them that God is their rock and security.

6. Beach Ball Toss

(You'll need a beach ball.)

As the rocks are drying, have the group stand in a circle.

Read aloud Isaiah 26:4b: **"Trust the Lord because he is our Rock forever."**

Ask kids to repeat the verse several times. Then bring out a beach ball. Ask who knows the first word of the verse. Toss the ball to one of those people. Ask that person to throw the ball to another person. He or she catches the ball, says the next word of the verse, and then throws it to another person, who says the next word of the verse, and so on until the verse is completed.

If a person catches the ball and can't say the next word of the verse, start the verse again from the beginning. Repeat the verse several times until the whole group knows it.

7. We're in God's Hands

Ask children to sing "He's Got the Whole World in His Hands." Sing the first verse, then for additional verses, sing the children's names in place of the phrase "the whole world." For example, "He's got Julie Smith in his hands." Sing until each child's name has been sung.

Close with prayer. Let kids take home their rocks as reminders to "Trust the Lord because he is our Rock forever."

by Ray and Cindy Peppers

I Like to Learn

Children spend a lot of time in school—a place of great influence. When kids like school, it can be a happy experience. When kids are unhappy about school, it can be a horrible experience. Helping children experience the adventure of learning can make school fun.

Use this lesson to help children experience ways school is fun and learning is important.

A POWERFUL PURPOSE

Children will explore the importance of school and discover that learning is important to Jesus.

A LOOK AT THE LESSON

1. Teacher for a Day (5 minutes)
2. Okay, Teachers (6 minutes)
3. Question Quest (6 minutes)
4. Jesus and Learning (6 minutes)
5. Learning Questions (6 minutes)
6. My School Emblem (8 minutes)
7. School Snacks (5 minutes)
8. Learning Song (3 minutes)

A SPRINKLING OF SUPPLIES

Gather a Bible, chalkboard and chalk, chairs, desk, cooked elbow macaroni, blindfolds, tape, finger paints, posterboard, water, towels, old shirts or aprons, newspapers, vanilla wafers, milk, cups, napkins, and a photocopy of the "Learning Cube" handout.

THE LIVELY LESSON

1. Teacher for a Day

(Set up the meeting area like a school classroom. Arrange chairs in rows and put a desk in front. Place a chalkboard behind the desk.)

Welcome children as they arrive and form groups of three. Ask all children to sit by their partners in the seats.

Say: **Guess what? For this activity you're going to be teacher of your class. You and your partners get to make one new rule about school. No rules like "No more homework" or "Recess all day," but good rules like "No talking without raising your hand" or "Be kind and helpful to others." You decide what new rule would make school better. You have a short time to decide. When you figure out your rule, you and your partners will act it out in front of the large group, and we'll try to guess.**

Help each group think of a rule and decide how to act it out. For example, for "No talking without raising your hand," kids each could simply place one hand over their mouth while they raise their other hand.

2. Okay, Teachers

Say: **Okay, teachers. Now's the time to act out our rules.**

Ask for a group to act out a rule first. Then ask the others to guess the rule. Write the new rule on the chalkboard. When each group has reported, ask:

● **How did you feel as you led the class?**

● **What was hardest about thinking of rules? easiest?**

● **Why are rules important at school?**

Say: **Being a teacher is hard. Teachers care about you and want you to learn as much as you can. Learning is important. Today we're going to talk a lot about school and learning.**

3. Question Quest

(You'll need a bowl of cooked elbow macaroni and a blindfold for each child.)

Blindfold all the children. Say: **Learning can be an exciting discovery. And we have to ask lots of questions to learn. I have a bowl with something in it. You have to ask me questions to figure out what it is. You might ask: "Is it red? Is it big? Is it alive?" But I can only respond "yes" or "no" to your questions. As soon as you think you know what's in the bowl, raise your hand. You can whisper your idea to me. But don't tell anyone else, because we want everyone to learn.**

Give kids time to ask questions blindly. Then say: **Now I'm going to let you smell what I have.** Take the bowl to each child to smell briefly, and let them ask more questions.

Say: **Now I'm going to let you touch what I have—but only with one finger.** Take the bowl to each child and answer questions. If children still haven't guessed what's in the bowl, say: **Now you can look at what I have. Take off your blindfolds!** Then ask:

● **What was hardest about guessing?**

● **How did asking questions help you learn what's in the bowl?**

● **How did you feel when one of your questions gave important information?**

● **How does asking questions help you learn?**

4. Jesus and Learning

(You'll need a Bible.)

Say: **There's a story in Luke about how important learning was to Jesus when he was 12 years old. Let's read about it. Every time you hear the words "questions," "listen" or "learn," stand up for a moment.**

Read aloud Luke 2:41-52 from a children's Bible, pausing at appropriate places long enough for kids to stand, then sit down. Then have kids follow the same instructions and say: **Even as a boy, Jesus wanted to learn everything he could from them. Learning was important to him. So he listened to his teachers and asked lots of questions.**

5. Learning Questions

(You'll need a photocopy of the "Learning Cube" handout. Cut out the diagram, then fold and tape the sides to make a cube.)

Gather the students in a circle. Tell them they're going to play a game called "Learning Questions." Each person will roll the cube. There's a question on each side. The person who rolls the cube will try to answer the question on top when the cube stops rolling.

Show students what to do by rolling the cube and answering the question. Then start with the person on your right. Go around the circle giving everyone a chance. Several children can answer the same question. Read the questions for the kids.

After you play a while, ask:

● **How do you feel after playing that game?**

● **What did you learn about others in our group?**

6. My School Emblem

(You'll need finger paints, posterboard, old shirts or aprons, newspaper in the painting area, and water and towels for cleanup.)

Gather students around the finger paints and posterboard. Ask them to cover their good clothes with the old shirts or aprons.

Encourage kids to use the supplies to design a symbol or picture of their favorite part of school. They could paint a book if their favorite part of school is reading. They could paint a design of numbers if their favorite part of school is math.

Clean up with the water and towels.

7. School Snacks

(You'll need vanilla wafers, milk, cups and napkins.)

Let the paintings dry while you eat refreshments. Serve students a school snack of vanilla wafers and milk.

8. Learning Song

When they finish eating, teach children this prayer song to the tune of "Are You Sleeping?":

I like learning.
I like learning.
Thank you, God.
Thank you, God.
Help me grow in school, now.
Help me grow in school, now.
A-amen.
A-amen.

by Mike Gillespie

LEARNING CUBE

Photocopy this handout. Cut out the shape along the solid lines. Fold along the dotted lines. Tape it to form a cube.

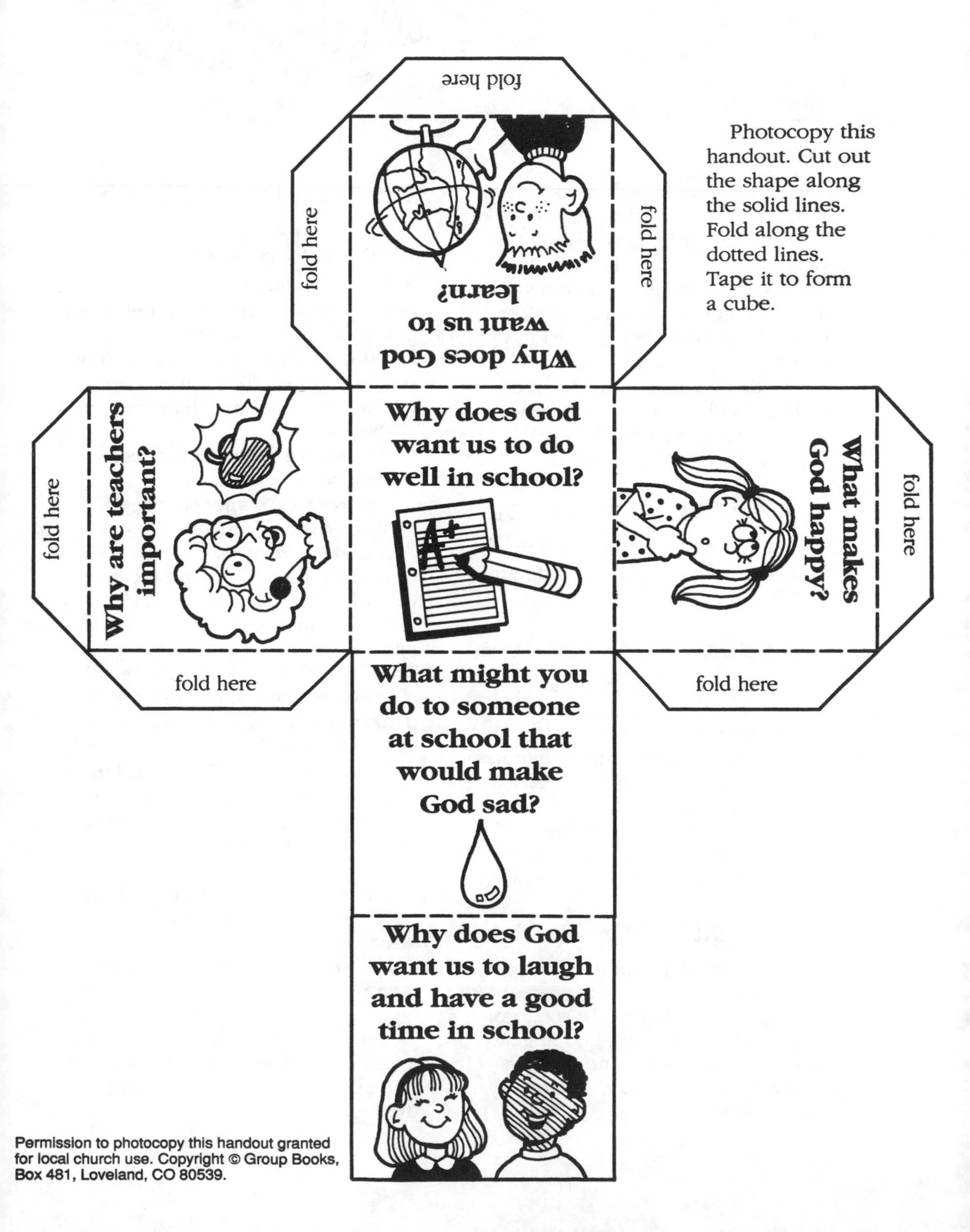

Permission to photocopy this handout granted for local church use. Copyright © Group Books, Box 481, Loveland, CO 80539.

I Am Special

A lot of our world's influences seem custom-designed to make us feel insignificant or ignored. Beautiful people in ads, beautiful homes, cars, clothes. Children are not exempt from these influences. They need all the help they can get to develop healthy self-esteem.

Use this lesson to encourage each child. Treat him or her as special. Reinforce that we are all special because God made us special.

A POWERFUL PURPOSE

Children will learn there's nobody else like them. They are unique and wonderful.

A LOOK AT THE LESSON

1. March to a Beat (3 minutes)
2. Butcher Paper Buddies (8 minutes)
3. Thumbprint Portraits (8 minutes)
4. Thumbprint Autograph Exchange (6 minutes)
5. What Can I Do? (5 minutes)
6. Balloon Buddies (6 minutes)
7. Finger Food Snacks (4 minutes)

A SPRINKLING OF SUPPLIES

Gather butcher paper; crayons; tape; scissors; safety pins; balloons; markers; ribbon; a Bible; 3×5 cards; stamp pad; water and a washcloth; and finger foods such as cheese and crackers, peanut butter on celery, or small sandwiches.

THE LIVELY LESSON

1. March to a Beat

Gather children in a circle after they enter the room. Tell them they're going to discover all kinds of things they can do, because God made each one of them special. Teach this chant chorus to a one-two, marching beat.

Chorus:

Are we God's special ones?
Yes, we are, uh huh.
Are we God's special ones?
Yes, we are, uh huh.

After kids memorize the words, have them practice saying it while marching in place. Have the kids say the chant, then tell them one body part and action they have to do. They'll do the action then repeat the chant chorus. Continue, using these parts and actions. Add more of your own actions and ideas.

Since we are God's special ones
Let me see you nod your head

(Pause while they do the action, then repeat chorus.)

Since we are God's special ones
Let me see you roll your shoulders

(Pause while they do the action, then repeat chorus.)

Since we are God's special ones
Let me see you wiggle your arms

(Pause while they do the action, then repeat chorus.)

Since we are God's special ones
Let me see you wave your hands
(Pause while they do the action, then repeat chorus.)

Since we are God's special ones
Let me see you turn around
(Repeat the chorus one last time.)

2. Butcher Paper Buddies

(You'll need a Bible, butcher paper, crayons, scissors and tape.)

Lay butcher paper on the floor. Use crayons to trace each person's body outline. Let kids each cut out their outline and color it. Have them color the paper buddy similar to what they're wearing.

As they're designing their buddies ask:

● **What body part do you think is most important?**

● **What would happen if we tried to use a foot to hear? an ear to eat? a toe to drink?**

● **What would our bodies look like if we only had one part, like a giant ear or nose?**

● **How would you feel if you didn't have one part of your body?**

● **Why do you think God made our bodies with so many different parts?**

Say: **Different body parts do different things. Similarly, each of us is special and different. God says we are like the body parts. Although we look different and can do different things, we all are important and necessary. No one else is like us anywhere in the world. Even people who look alike, such as identical twins, are different inside.**

Ask kids to keep decorating silently while you read about our specialness in 1 Corinthians 12:14-27.

After kids have decorated and cut out their body buddies, tape them all around your meeting room, like life-size paper dolls. Let children enjoy their creations throughout the lesson.

3. Thumbprint Portraits

(You'll need 3×5 cards, crayons, a stamp pad, water and a washcloth.)

Say: **We are special and unique. No two of us are alike. Just look at all the butcher paper buddies around the room. We're like thumbprints. Did you know that no two thumbprints are alike? Let's see.**

Give each child a 3×5 card. On the top of each card, write "I am thumbody special." Ask kids each to write their name at the bottom of their card and help those who can't.

Have children each carefully press their thumb on the stamp pad and print it on their card. Wash thumbs with water and a washcloth.

Blow on the prints to dry. Have kids compare their thumbprints and see how they're each different. Let kids each make a thumbprint portrait by designing the thumbprint as a head and adding a body to it. You design one and show kids as an example. The "Thumbody Special" diagram shows how one can look.

4. Thumbprint Autograph Exchange

(You'll need safety pins and crayons.)

Let kids mingle around the room and sign their initials to each other's card. Encourage kids to get each person's autograph. (If you don't mind a little more mess, let kids add their thumbprints to each other's cards.)

Use the safety pins and help kids each pin their card on their shirt. Then ask:

- **How does it feel to know you're special?**
- **What special things do you see in other people in our class?**

5. What Can I Do?

Say: **Each body part is made to do something special. Point to each body part as I say its specialty.** Mention each of the following specialities, and wait for kids to point to the appropriate body part:

Feeling—hands
Talking—mouth
Seeing—eyes
Hearing—ears
Walking—feet
Thinking—head

Say: **Now I'm going to read a short story about how we can use these different body parts to do nice things for other people. Whenever I say something we can do, point to the body part involved.** When kids understand, read the following, pausing between each action for kids to point.

God made each person to be special. We can clap . . . say "Thank you" . . . think nice thoughts . . . look for ways to help people . . . listen to someone who is sad . . . run to help someone . . . hug someone . . . say "I love God" . . . listen to our parents . . . go for walks with friends . . . laugh.

6. Balloon Buddies

(You'll need balloons, ribbons and markers.)

Say: **Let's make one more reminder of what a unique, special, one-of-a-kind person you are.**

Inflate the balloons and give one to each child. Hand out markers, and ask children each to draw their own face on their balloon. On the back of the balloon, write or have the children write "I Am Special." Tell them not to press too hard or they'll pop the balloons.

Tie colorful ribbons to the balloons and let kids take them home.

7. Finger Food Snacks

(You'll need finger foods for snacks, such as cheese and crackers, peanut butter or cheese spread on celery, or small sandwiches.)

Ask kids to form a circle. Pass out the finger foods. Before children eat, have them say: "Thanks, God, for making me special."

by Karen M. Ball

Part 2: A Lively Look at My Relationships

Who Do We Appreciate?

Children love to have parties and receive gifts. But they also love to give things to others, because it makes them feel good.

Create a festive atmosphere for this lesson. Help children see there are simple and fun ways to show appreciation. Emphasize that appreciation is one gift that'll make the giver, the receiver and God feel good.

A POWERFUL PURPOSE

Children will understand why it's good to show appreciation to others.

A LOOK AT THE LESSON

1. Decoration Sensation (6 minutes)
2. Gift Giving and Singing (6 minutes)
3. What Makes Parties Fun? (3 minutes)
4. Love Comes From God (4 minutes)
5. A Gift for You (4 minutes)
6. Give a Hug (3 minutes)
7. Center of Affirmation (5 minutes)
8. We Appreciate Snacks (6 minutes)
9. Showing Appreciation (7 minutes)

A SPRINKLING OF SUPPLIES

Fill a sack with party decorations such as streamers, balloons, party hats, noisemakers, banners and festive tablecloths. You'll also need a bag filled with wrapped, inexpensive gifts such as pencils, stickers and magnets. You'll need a chalkboard and chalk, a bag of Hershey's Kisses, construction paper, crayons, glue, scissors, a Bible and one decorated cupcake for each person.

THE LIVELY LESSON

1. Decoration Sensation

(You'll need a paper sack filled with decorations such as streamers, balloons, party hats, noisemakers, banners and festive tablecloths.)

Show children the plain paper bag when they come in the room. Say: **We're going to talk about appreciation today. To appreciate means to be grateful or glad or thankful. In a moment, you're going to appreciate me for what I'm going to let out of this bag.**

Empty the sack's contents on the floor and show the kids all the party decorations. Say: **Instant party!**

Give everyone one decoration. Have kids each contribute to decorating the entire room. Afterward say: **I really appreciate each one of you. You did a great job decorating this room. Our party today is to celebrate each one of you as a person. I appreciate God creating you!** Ask:

- **How does it feel to know you could contribute to the decorating?**
- **When do people tell you they appreciate what you do?**

2. Gift Giving and Singing

(You'll need a bag filled with small wrapped, inexpensive gifts such as pencils, stickers or magnets. Make sure you have one for each person.)

After decorating, have kids form a circle in the center of the room. Sing upbeat and happy songs such as "If You're Happy and You Know It." Or, sing some affirmation songs such as "Jesus Loves Me." Have kids each sing their name in place of the word "me."

Bring out the bag of small wrapped gifts. Let children reach in and take one. As they take one say: **I appreciate you, (name).**

After all kids have a gift, let them open them. Then ask:

● **How does receiving a gift make you feel?**

● **What are other times you've felt appreciated by parents or friends?**

● **When you appreciate people, what kinds of gifts do you give?**

3. What Makes Parties Fun?

Go around the room and let each person describe his or her gift. After everyone shares, ask:

● **Why are parties so much fun?**

● **What's the best part of a party?**

● **How many of you like gifts the best?**

Say: **There are lots of reasons to have parties. Parties let people know we like them. And they celebrate something special that's happened to someone we like. It makes God happy when we show we appreciate each other. He wants us to enjoy being together.**

4. Love Comes From God

(Write each word of 1 John 4:7-8 on a separate small piece of paper. Place each piece of paper under a party hat. Scramble the words so they aren't in order.)

Tell kids that God wants us to appreciate each other and love each other. He tells us in 1 John 4:7-8 "Love each other, because love comes from God."

Have kids repeat the verse several times until they know it. Then show them the hats. Take turns lifting up a hat and seeing which word is under it. Kids try to find the first word to the verse, then the second word, and so on until they discover the entire verse.

5. A Gift for You

(You'll need a bag of Hershey's Kisses.)

Ask: **Why do we give gifts?** Answers could be to show we like someone, to make someone feel good or to celebrate something.

Have children pair up. Give each person a Hershey's Kiss. Say: **Give your Hershey's Kiss to your partner and say what you appreciate about him or her. For example, you may appreciate that person's smiles or friendliness.**

Let kids exchange Hershey's Kisses and affirmations. Participate yourself, making sure everyone's included.

6. Give a Hug

Say: **We can give each other all kinds of wonderful gifts. It's good to give someone a gift you know he or she will really enjoy. There are some gifts you can give people, though, that can't be wrapped up and put in a box. They are gifts people really like too. Can you guess what they are?**

Give children time to think of things such as hugs, handshakes, kisses, smiles and encouragement.

Tell kids they have one minute to give each person in the room a hug or a handshake for a gift. Call time when a minute is up!

● **What was it like to give lots of people a hug or a handshake?**

● **How did it feel to have others give you a hug or handshake?**

7. Center of Affirmation

(You'll need a party hat. Set up chairs in a circle. Put one chair in the center. Place a party hat on the chair.)

Tell children that another good gift is appreciation. Appreciation is letting people know what you like about them. It's a part of loving each other. You can show appreciation many ways such as sending special notes, saying thank you or giving hugs.

Tell kids to sit in the circle of chairs. Sit in the middle and put on the party hat. Say that they'll play an appreciation game. One at a time a person sits in the center chair and puts on the party hat. Kids in the circle each say one thing they appreciate about the center person.

Let everyone have a chance to be in the "Center of Affirmation" (yourself included). Affirm visitors for ways they've already contributed to the class.

8. We Appreciate Snacks

(You'll need decorated cupcakes.)

Hold hands and pray: **Thank you, God, for giving us people to appreciate. Please help us remember to love people by showing appreciation to someone every day. Help us remember to appreciate you for all the things you have done for us. In Jesus' name. Amen**

Give a colorful cupcake to one person and say: **Love each other.** Give a cupcake to another person and say: **Love comes from God.** Do this until everyone has a cupcake. Enjoy and appreciate the snacks!

9. Showing Appreciation

(You'll need a chalkboard and chalk, the party decorations, construction paper, glue, crayons and scissors.)

Ask children to name people they appreciate, such as moms, dads, brothers, sisters, friends, grandparents, teachers and pastors.

Tell kids they're each going to make a card for one special person of their choice. Brainstorm words or pictures of appreciation they could write or draw. For example, "Thanks for making me happy!" or "I love you!" Write words on the chalkboard so they can copy them.

Show kids the supplies and give each person a piece of construction paper. Tell them to take down and use any of the party decorations and supplies to design a card for their special person. For example, they could cut some shapes from a colorful streamer and glue the shapes on the front of a folded piece of construction paper. They could tape a balloon inside the card and write, "Thanks for being my friend."

After the cards are finished, have kids show them and tell about the special people who'll receive them. Close with prayer, thanking God for all the special people he has given us. Encourage children to show appreciation through the coming week.

by Karen M. Ball

The Gift of Friendship

As children grow older, their desire for friendship grows. Children need friends. Use this lesson to help kids make new friends. Offer children the good news that God wants us to have lots of friends.

A Powerful Purpose

Children will experience how new friends are a gift from God.

A Look at the Lesson

1. Find a Friend (3 minutes)
2. New Friend for a Day Necklace (5 minutes)
3. More Friends (2 minutes)
4. Build a Friend (5 minutes)
5. Friends Come in All Sizes, Shapes and Colors (4 minutes)
6. Jesus and His Friends (6 minutes)
7. Have a Heart (8 minutes)
8. Friendship Snack (5 minutes)

A Sprinkling of Supplies

Gather a Bible, photocopies of the handout, paper, crayons, yarn, paper plates, hole punch, tape, construction paper, scissors, potatoes, tempera paint, bowls, old shirts or aprons, ice cream cones, ice cream and a scoop.

The Lively Lesson

1. Find a Friend

(Cut several pairs of paper strips in 1-, 2-, 3-, 4-, 5- and 6-inch lengths depending on the number of kids. You'll need two identical-length strips per pair of kids.)

As children arrive, hand each one a strip of paper. Ask them each to find a friend by looking for the other person whose strip of paper is exactly the same length. When they find the person they should sit down together.

Say: **Today we're going to talk about friends. You're now sitting with your "New Friend for a Day." Tell each other your name and which flavor of ice cream you like best: vanilla, chocolate or strawberry. Remember your friend's flavor, because you'll need to know it later.**

2. New Friend for a Day Necklace

(Cut a 20-inch length of yarn for each person. Use a hole punch to place a hole near the edge of each paper plate, preparing one plate for each person. Set up a table with the crayons, yarn and paper plates.)

Tell children they're each going to make a "New Friend for a Day Necklace." Ask kids each to take a paper plate and draw a picture of their new friend. They also should draw a picture of an ice cream cone and color it their new friend's favorite flavor.

After they finish, help them stick a piece of yarn through the hole and tie it. Ask kids to hold onto the necklaces and not wear them yet.

3. More Friends

Say: **We're all friends in this room. So, find two other people and ask them to print their names on the other side of your paper necklace. Then, hang the friendship necklace around your neck.**

If you have younger children in your group who're still learning to print their names, help them write their names or ask them to print their first initial.

4. Build a Friend

(Cut body parts out of construction paper as illustrated in the "Friendship Parts" diagram. Have tape and markers available.)

Give the different body parts to six different children. Have the class work together to piece the body together and tape it on a wall. Tape a blank sheet above the figure and write "A friend is someone who . . ." Read the words as you write them.

Say: **Think of ways to complete the statement I just wrote on the paper. You might say, "A friend is someone who spends time with me" or "A friend is someone who's fun to play with."**

Write the responses on the construction paper figure. Ask:

- **How many of these things do you do for your friends?**
- **Which ones are most important to you?**

Say: **Remember, friends do things that help us. Also, don't forget that your parents are your good friends too.**

5. Friends Come in All Sizes, Shapes and Colors

(You'll need scissors and various colors of construction paper.)

Have kids each cut out three different shapes—a circle, a triangle and a square. Use a different color for each shape. Kids can cut the shapes any size they want.

Demonstrate first, then let the kids do it. It's okay if some children are just learning to cut. Odd shapes will simply reinforce your point that friends come in different sizes and shapes.

Gather all the different sizes of shapes and spread them out in front of the group. Gather all of the circles and say: **Look at all these circles. They are different sizes and colors but they're still circles. The same goes for the triangles and squares. New friends are like that. Sometimes new friends are tall or short. Sometimes they're a different color. Sometimes they're girls or boys. But they're still friends.**

6. Jesus and His Friends

(You'll need a Bible.)

Say: **Did you ever wonder if Jesus had friends? Sure he did. Lots of them. But his closest friends were the disciples. We're going to read about and then act out the time when Jesus met four of his new friends.**

Read the story from Mark 1:16-20.

Appoint four children to be Simon, Andrew, James and John. Send Simon and Andrew to one side of the room and James and John to the other side of the room. Tell the rest of the kids they'll be Jesus. They're going to visit Simon and Andrew, then James and John. Lead the group to where Simon and Andrew are standing.

Have the kids repeat these words and actions after you.

Hey, Simon.

Come be my new friend. (Motion for Simon to join the group.)

Help me tell people about God.

Hey, Andrew.

Come be my new friend. (Motion for Andrew to join the group.)

Help me tell people about God.

(Everybody walks to where James and John are standing.)

Hey, James.

Come be my new friend. (Motion for James to join the group.)

Help me tell people about God.

Hey, John.

Come be my new friend. (Motion for John to join the group.)

Help me tell people about God.

Sit in a circle; then ask:

- **How did it feel to welcome others to be friends?**
- **Why do you think Jesus asked these four men to be his disciples and new friends?**

Allow time for discussion, then say: **Jesus wanted Simon, Andrew, James and John to help him tell people the good news that God loved them. Friends help us share God's love with one another. God wants us to have new friends. God also wants each of us to be a new friend to someone.**

7. Have a Heart

(Cut several potatoes in half and carve hearts on the cut side so they extend 1/4 inch. Pour small amounts of different-color tempera paint in bowls. Cover the table and floor to protect against stray paint. You'll also need old shirts or aprons, photocopies of the "A Friend Loves You All the Time" handout and crayons. Place all of these items on a table.)

Take the group to the table. Cover kids' good clothes with the old shirts or aprons. Read aloud the handout title: "A Friend Loves You All the Time." Encourage kids each to color their handout with crayons, then dip the potato hearts into the paint and make more hearts on the handout. Let kids take the handouts home.

8. Friendship Snack

(You'll need ice cream cones, an ice cream scoop, and vanilla, chocolate and strawberry ice cream.)

Gather the children around the ice cream. Say that you'll prepare the ice cream cones. They'll get a cone to give to their new friends, depending on his or her favorite flavor.

After friends serve each other, let everyone eat.

Gather in a circle and ask:

- **What did you learn about your new friend?**
- **How can what you learned help you with other friendships?**

Close with a prayer, thanking God for new friends.

by Mike Gillespie

Permission to photocopy this handout granted for local church use. Copyright © Group Books, Box 481, Loveland, CO 80539.

Love Goes Around

Children in kindergarten through the third grade are making friends with children at school and at church. They're forming peer groups that are important to them.

"Socially, the eight-year-old's interest is with the peer group," write Barbara Bolton, Charles T. Smith and Wes Haystead, authors of *Everything You Want to Know About Teaching Children*. "It is important [for children] to fit in and belong." Use this lesson to teach them that good friendships are friendships filled with love.

A Powerful Purpose

Children will learn the importance of loving friends.

A Look at the Lesson

1. Animal Pairs (4 minutes)
2. Friendship Tablecloth (6 minutes)
3. Friends Stick Together (4 minutes)
4. Double Whammy (7 minutes)
5. Jesus: The Best Friend of All (3 minutes)
6. Turn Those Frowns Upside Down (5 minutes)
7. A Good Samaritan, a Good Friend (5 minutes)
8. Friendship Prayer (1 minute)

A Sprinkling of Supplies

Gather tape, newsprint, crayons, plastic knives, crackers, peanut butter, two soft foam balls, paper plates and a Bible.

The Lively Lesson

1. Animal Pairs

Photocopy and cut apart the "Animals" handout so each child can have one animal. Include two of each animal. For example, if you have 10 kids, you might use two cats, two dogs, two birds, two cows and two elephants.

When children arrive, give each child an animal from the handout. Tell kids to look at the animals and not tell anyone what they have. Have children then walk around the room making the noise of their animal until they find the other person making the same noise.

After everyone has found a partner, ask:

- **What do you and your partner have in common as the animal, such as trunks, beaks, a bark?**
- **Why didn't you pair up with another animal?**

Then say: **You and your partner have something in common. And the same can be said about the people you spend time with. You play with kids who like doing the same things you do.**

2. Friendship Tablecloth

(Secure white newsprint on a table with tape. You'll also need crayons.)

Gather the children around the white paper tablecloth. Give children crayons and tell them to draw pictures of activities they do with friends. For example, they may draw children riding bicycles,

ANIMALS

Photocopy and cut apart the animal cards below.

Permission to photocopy this handout granted for local church use. Copyright © Group Books, Box 481, Loveland, CO 80539.

talking on the telephone or swinging at the playground.

When children finish ask:

● **What did you draw?**

● **What do you enjoy doing best with your friends? Why?**

Then say: **When we spend time with friends, we like to do things together that make us happy. And when we're happy, Jesus is happy.**

3. Friends Stick Together

(You'll need plastic knives, crackers and a jar of peanut butter.)

Have children take a seat around the table. Give them each a plastic knife and cracker. Place a jar of peanut butter on the table for kids to spread on their crackers. Explain they can't eat their own peanut butter crackers; instead they must give them to someone else at the table.

As children eat the crackers they've received, say: **Good friends stick together—just like peanut butter sticks on the cracker. And friends are good friends when they do nice things for us.**

4. Double Whammy

(You may need to go outside or to a larger room to play this game. You'll need two soft foam balls.)

Before you play, make sure the children know each other's names. Get two soft foam balls. Set boundaries no more than 20 yards square. Explain you're going to play "Double Whammy," a game where two children will each throw a ball into the air and call out another child's name at the same time. The two whose names are called must each try to catch the ball. Children who don't get called must run away from the ball.

When the two children whose names were called catch their balls, they can each throw the ball to try to hit someone below the knees. If a child is hit, he or she then takes the ball and gets to throw the ball into the air and say another child's name. If a child misses, he or she gets to throw the ball into the air and say a child's name. Children cannot throw their balls into the air until both children with the two balls are ready.

After the game, ask:

● **How did it feel to have your name called?**

● **What did you like best: throwing the ball in the air, catching the ball, throwing the ball at someone or having the ball thrown at you? Why?**

Say: **Friends like to play together, but they don't like to hurt each other. Friends like it when everybody is happy.**

5. Jesus: The Best Friend of All

Say: **Jesus also likes it when we're happy. He's sad when we're sad. And Jesus loves each one of us very much and is our friend.**

Read aloud John 15:14: **"And you are my friends if you do what I command you."** (TEV)

Then sing this song to the tune of "Jesus Loves Me."

And you are my friends if you
Do what I command you to.
And you are my friends if you
Do what I command you to.

Yes, Jesus loves me,
Yes, Jesus loves me,
Yes, Jesus loves me,
And says he is my friend.

6. Turn Those Frowns Upside Down

(You'll need a paper plate and crayons for each person.)

Give children each a paper plate and a crayon. Have the children each draw a sad face on one side of their plate and a happy face on the opposite side of the plate.

Say: **I'm going to read you different things that can happen. Depending on how you or the other person mentioned would feel, either hold up your sad face or happy face.**

Then read these situations:

- **I fall down and skin my knee.**
- **A friend gives me a bandage.**
- **I fall off my bicycle.**
- **A friend loses her favorite stuffed animal.**
- **Jesus says he loves me.**
- **Someone in my class says he's my best friend.**
- **My brother yells at me.**
- **My sister hugs me.**
- **Jesus is my friend.**

Then say: **Jesus wants us to be happy. And whenever we're sad, we can tell our good friend Jesus how we feel. Take home your happy faces and hang them on your wall to remind you to be happy about the good friends you have and the good friend you have in Jesus.**

7. A Good Samaritan, a Good Friend

(Draw a large happy face on a piece of newsprint and tape it to one wall. You'll also need a Bible.)

Read aloud the parable of the Good Samaritan in Luke 10:25-37. As you read the story, have children act it out as if they were the man traveling from Jerusalem to Jericho. Choose three other children to act the parts of the priest, the Levite and the Samaritan.

For example, have all the children except the three who are acting the part of the priest, Levite and Samaritan, walk around the room at the beginning of the story. Then have them fall to the floor when the robbers beat them up. Have them lie on the floor.

Then have the one child acting as the priest walk by all the children. Have the child acting as the Levite walk past all the children. Then have the Samaritan tend to all the children's wounds and help each up individually and bring them to an inn, which you have designated by a big happy face taped to one wall.

After the story ask:

- **Who was a good friend?**
- **Who wasn't a good friend?**
- **How did it feel to lie on the floor and have two people walk past you and not help you?**
- **How did it feel when you were helped?**

Say: **Good friends take care of each other. They don't walk by when you're hurt. Instead they stop to help you. That's the kind of friend we should all be for others.**

8. Friendship Prayer

Say: **Before you go to bed each night, thank Jesus for all the friends you have. Then thank Jesus for being your friend.**

Have children bow their heads and fold their hands. Pray, thanking Jesus for friends. (Name each individual child during the thank-you prayer.)

by Jolene L. Roehlkepartain

Solving Problems With Forgiveness

As children's social experiences increase, so do problems. Conflicts arise daily within families and among friends. Problem-solving techniques teach the resolution of conflict by facing the situation and verbally expressing feelings. As Christians, however, we take this one step further. As Jesus has forgiven us, we must do the same. When we wrong others, we must learn to say "I'm sorry." When someone wrongs us, we must learn to say "I forgive you."

Use this lesson to let children practice forgiving and seeing the good in others.

A POWERFUL PURPOSE

Children will solve friendship problems by practicing forgiveness.

A LOOK AT THE LESSON

1. Let's Get Together (5 minutes)
2. Mirror Me (5 minutes)
3. Partner Problem-Solving (7 minutes)
4. Chain of Forgiveness (7 minutes)
5. Which One Is Missing? (6 minutes)
6. Words Work (5 minutes)
7. Giant Hug (7 minutes)
8. Sharing a Snack (8 minutes)
9. Recipe for Friendship (4 minutes)

A SPRINKLING OF SUPPLIES

Gather a Bible, construction paper, glue, crayons, one bean bag (or crumpled piece of paper) for every two people, butcher paper, pencils, scissors, peanut butter, jelly, bread, napkins, plastic knives and photocopies of the handout.

THE LIVELY LESSON

1. Let's Get Together

Greet the children, then gather and sit in a circle. Say: **The Bible tells us to be kind to each other and forgive each other. Right now we're going to practice being kind to each other.**

Ask each child to say something kind about the person on his or her right. For example "I like you" or "You're fun."

Lead the children in this song to the tune of "The Farmer in the Dell."

(Clasp neighbors' shoulders.)
Let's get together now.
Let's get together now.
You are my friends, my friends.
Let's get together now.

(Clasp neighbors' hands gently rocking back and forth.)
Let's love each other now.

Let's love each other now.
You are my friends, my friends.
Let's love each other now.

2. Mirror Me

Form pairs by having kids each grab hands with a person beside them. Tell the partners they're going to play a game to help them recognize others' feelings. Say: **One person in each pair will pretend to be a mirror. The other person is an actor. I'll name an emotion, and the actor must act it out. The mirror must copy or "mirror" the actor. Ready?**

Name emotions such as love, happiness, fear, loneliness, confusion, worry and sadness. After a variety of feelings have been explored, ask kids to switch roles so that mirrors become actors and actors become mirrors. Then ask:

- **What made the experience fun? hard?**
- **Why is it important to know what others are feeling?**

3. Partner Problem-Solving

Say: **I'm going to read some situations. After each one, talk to your partner about how the situation makes you feel. Then talk about what you could do to make the situation better or solve the problem.**

Use these situations, and add some of your own:

- **A friend says she'll pick you up at your house one morning so you can walk to school together. She never comes. You start to walk alone. You see her. She's walking with another friend and pretends not to notice you.**
  How do you feel?
  How can you make this situation better?
- **A friend has a birthday party. Everyone in the neighborhood is invited, except you.**
  How do you feel?
  How can you make this situation better?
- **Your sister made a big mess in the basement. Your mom thinks you did it, and she sends you to your room. No matter what you say, she thinks you did it. Your sister doesn't stick up for you.**
  How do you feel?
  How can you make this situation better?

4. Chain of Forgiveness

(You'll need 1×4 strips of construction paper, glue and crayons.)

Ask kids to think about times family or friends may have hurt them. Provide the strips of paper, crayons and glue. Instruct them to write one name per strip of paper. Help the children who are just learning to write. Glue the strips together to make a chain for the whole class. As kids attach each name, encourage kids to forgive that person.

Hang the forgiveness chain on one wall of the room.

5. Which One Is Missing?

(Cut nine footprints out of paper. On each footprint, write one word from Ephesians 4:32: "Be kind to one another, forgiving each other.")

Read this paraphrase of Ephesians 4:32 to the kids: "Be kind to one another, forgiving each other." Place the footprints in order on the floor as you read each word. Reread the verse several times.

Give each child an opportunity to remove one of the footprints while the others' backs are turned. Then ask the others to turn back around and try to guess which word/footprint is missing.

After kids seem to know the verse, scramble the words and let the children unscramble them.

6. Words Work

(You'll need a bean bag or a crumpled piece of paper for every two people.)

Children need practice using the phrases "I'm sorry" and "I forgive you." Give each pair a bean bag or crumpled piece of paper.

One person tosses the bean bag to the other and says, "I'm sorry." The other child catches it and says, "I forgive you." The pattern is repeated, giving each child practice saying both.

After some tossing time say: **These words are more than a game. They help you solve problem situations. They show that you care.** Ask kids to brainstorm how they might use the words to solve problems.

7. Giant Hug

(Each child will need a pencil and a 5×30 piece of paper cut as shown in the "Giant Hug" diagram.)

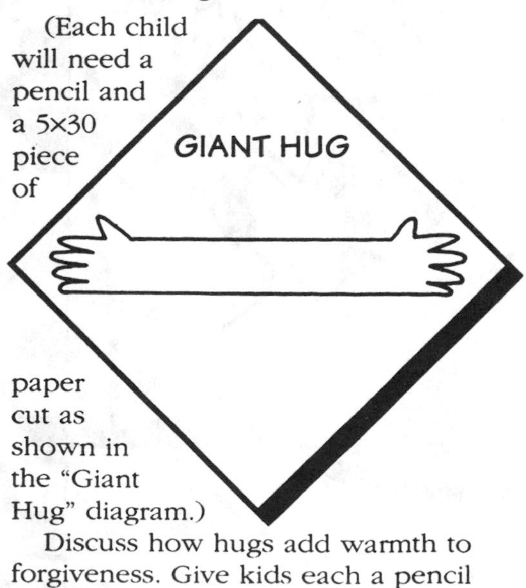

Discuss how hugs add warmth to forgiveness. Give kids each a pencil and a "Giant Hug" piece of paper. Have them each write on one side "I'm sorry" and on the other side "I forgive you." Again, help the ones who are learning to write.

Invite the children to take turns wrapping their paper hugs around each other.

8. Sharing a Snack

(You'll need peanut butter, jelly, bread, plastic knives and napkins. You can let kids make their own sandwiches, or you can make them ahead of time and place each sandwich in a plastic bag.)

Have kids each make a sandwich and divide it into fourths. Have kids each share three pieces with three friends. No one can end up with more than four pieces. When kids each have four pieces (one of their own and three others) join hands and pray: "Thank you, Jesus, for helping us learn to share with others. Help us also learn to forgive others. Amen."

Eat and enjoy!

9. Recipe for Friendship

(You'll need crayons and a photocopy of the "Recipe to Be a Loving Friend and Family Member" handout for each person.)

Give each child a photocopy of the "Recipe to Be a Loving Friend and Family Member" handout and crayons. Let kids color the handout. Encourage each child to take it home for the entire family to see.

Close by singing the opening song. Add the following verse:

(Hold hands in a circle.)

Let's forgive each other now.
Let's forgive each other now.
You are my friends, my friends.
Let's forgive each other now.

by Jane P. Wilke

Permission to photocopy this handout granted for local church use. Copyright © Group Books, Box 481, Loveland, CO 80539.

Can I Help You?

Helping others fulfills two important needs for children: the need for accomplishment and the need for self-worth. Helping others, however, must be seen as more than a chore. Serving others can be fun and rewarding.

Use this lesson to give kids a desire to help neighbors, friends, family and others.

A POWERFUL PURPOSE

Children will discover practical ways to help others—like Jesus helped his disciples by washing their feet.

A LOOK AT THE LESSON

1. Let Me Help You (5 minutes)
2. A Story About Help (7 minutes)
3. Blind Scavenger Hunt (8 minutes)
4. Helping Questions (4 minutes)
5. Ways to Help (6 minutes)
6. Helping Coupons (6 minutes)
7. Trust Train to Treats (5 minutes)

A SPRINKLING OF SUPPLIES

Gather paper grocery bags; masking tape; a bucket of warm water, a washcloth, a towel; photocopies of the handout; crayons; newsprint; markers; blindfolds; a Bible; a stapler and staples; and snacks such as apples, oranges, bananas, and crackers and cheese.

THE LIVELY LESSON

1. Let Me Help You

(You'll need 10 to 15 paper grocery bags. Place two parallel lines of masking tape on the floor on opposite ends of your room.)

Welcome the kids and tell them they're going to learn about helping others—first by running a fun race.

Form teams of no more than 10. Each relay team will need five grocery bags. Bring extra bags in case some are destroyed during the race.

Have teams line up at one masking-tape line. Form pairs within each team. Have partners choose which person is to lead and which person is to put a paper grocery bag on each leg, each arm, and on his or her head.

On "go," have the leaders safely guide their partners to the masking-tape line across the room. Once they reach that line, have partners switch roles: the leaders wear the sacks; the sack-wearers lead. Have them head back to their team and tag the next partners, who repeat the process. Remind children to be careful to make sure they guide their partners safely.

All team members must complete the race. The first team to cross the finish line wins.

2. A Story About Help

(You'll need a Bible, a bucket of warm water, a washcloth and a towel.)

Say: **It's important for us to help**

each other. The Bible tells about a time when Jesus helped other people by washing their feet. Read aloud John 13:4-15. Then ask volunteers to take off their shoes and socks. Wash and dry each volunteer's feet. (If you have a large group, have another adult help.)

As you wash feet, talk about ways children can help each other—like Jesus washed his disciples' feet. Have kids brainstorm ideas. When you've washed all the volunteers' feet, have them put their shoes and socks back on. Ask:

- **What did it feel like to have me wash your feet?**
- **How do you feel when others help you?**
- **How do you feel when you help others?**

3. Blind Scavenger Hunt

(You'll need several blindfolds.)

Say: **We just heard a Bible story about a person who needed help and another person who offered help. We're going to learn more about helping by participating in a "Blind Scavenger Hunt."**

Blindfold several volunteers. Instruct the children without blindfolds to sit down in a corner of the room and watch. Then tell the blindfolded kids: **I'm going to name an item for you to find. It's in the room. You have to find it by yourself. Blindfolded. No help. Are you ready?** Choose any item such as a potted plant or a marker or a trash can.

Allow a minute for this attempt, then pair a sighted person with each blindfolded one. Have pairs find another item.

4. Helping Questions

(You'll need newsprint and a marker.)

Have the blindfolded kids take off their blindfolds. Gather in a circle and ask:

- **Which was the easiest way to find the object—blindfolded and by yourself or with a seeing partner? Why?**
- **What was hardest about the scavenger hunt? Why?**
- **For those who helped find the object, how did you feel helping?**
- **For those who received help finding the object, how did you feel?**
- **What are ways we can help parents? brothers or sisters? school friends? our church?**

Write the responses to the last question on newsprint. Ideas could include helping parents clean the house, helping babysit a little brother or sister, helping a friend study, helping a teacher pass out papers.

5. Ways to Help

Say: **We're going to create skits about ways to help others, but first we each need to find a partner.** Divide into pairs by having kids say these words one at a time, "Help, others, help, others . . . " All "helps" find an "other" to be a partner with.

Reread the newsprint list of ways to help. Have pairs develop a skit to show one way of helping. For example, one partner could pantomime sweeping and the other could pantomime dusting for "Helping parents clean the house."

Let all pairs act out their skit while others guess the action.

You might want to take an instant-print picture of each helping action. Post the pictures on a bulletin board titled "We Help Others."

Another option is to videotape the skits. Children love to see themselves on television!

6. Helping Coupons

(You'll need crayons, photocopies of the "Helping Coupon" handout, and a stapler and staples.)

Give children each crayons and several "Helping Coupon" handouts. Read the handout, then reread some of the ways to help.

Ask kids each to choose one person they want to make a coupon book for. It could be a parent, sister, brother, friend or teacher. Help them each write the person's name on each coupon's top line. Help kids sign their own names on the second line. Then have them draw in the space provided three to six ways to help that person—one drawing per coupon. Staple their coupons together to form a book.

Encourage kids to take the coupon books home and give them to the person to use this week.

7. Trust Train to Treats

(You'll need snacks set on a table. Try healthy snacks such as apples, oranges, bananas, crackers and cheese.)

Say: **Everyone line up in a straight line behind me. Now place your hands on the shoulders of the person in front of you. Are you all hooked in a train? Now close your eyes. Don't peek. You have to trust me to help you find your way to the treats.**

Lead the line on a wandering path to the treat table, then let kids open their eyes and eat the treats.

Remind children that God wants each of us to help others. Say a brief prayer, asking God to help us remember to think of others and help those around us.

by Patti Chromey

HELPING COUPON

To: ______________________________

From: ______________________________

I will help:

____

____

____

____

____

____

____

____

____

____

Satisfaction guaranteed!

Permission to photocopy this handout granted for local church use. Copyright © Group Books, Box 481, Loveland, CO 80539.

ACCEPTING OTHERS

Children are beginning to notice differences in people, such as disabilities, ethnicity, family heritage, behavior. However, children have not yet developed strong prejudices that often form barriers among teenagers and adults.

Use this lesson to help children understand that people are different, and develop a sensitivity and acceptance for others.

A POWERFUL PURPOSE

Children will understand and accept people who are different from them.

A LOOK AT THE LESSON

1. Circles or Triangles: Who's Best? (8 minutes)
2. Sack Trade (5 minutes)
3. Jesus and the Leper (8 minutes)
4. Different or the Same? (4 minutes)
5. It's Okay to Be Different (6 minutes)
6. Hurting Others (5 minutes)
7. Accepting Others (3 minutes)
8. Snack in a Sack (5 minutes)

A SPRINKLING OF SUPPLIES

Gather a Bible, construction paper, paper grocery bags, crayons, pencils, glue, newsprint, paper, a trash can, a coin, and fruit or candy in small paper sacks.

THE LIVELY LESSON

1. Circles or Triangles: Who's Best?

(Prepare a large grocery bag for each child as shown in the "Different Bags" diagram. Turn the bag upside down and cut a hole in the top and each side for a head and arms to slip through. Cut a slit up the middle to the head hole. Also cut several yellow circles and red triangles from construction paper. You'll also need glue.)

DIFFERENT BAGS

As kids arrive, welcome them and give them each a prepared paper sack. Tell half of the children to glue the yellow circles on their sacks. Tell the other half to glue on the red triangles.

2. Sack Trade

When kids finish, ask them to put on their sacks and gather in a circle. Tell them today's topic is differences. Say: **Sometimes it's hard to like people who seem different from us. They may go to a different**

school, wear different clothes, speak a different language or be from a different country. Sometimes differences cause problems. Right now half of our group is different from the other half. I wonder which group is better? I'm not going to tell you which group is "best," I'm going to let you decide. I'm going to give you a chance to trade your sack with someone if you feel he or she has a better sign or a better color. Some of you may want to keep the sack you're wearing. The only rule is that both of you must agree to trade. No tearing off any sacks. You have two minutes to trade.

After the trading, ask the groups to sit down with their "own kind." Ask how they decided to trade. What did they think made one sack better than the others? design? quality craftsmanship? guesswork?

3. Jesus and the Leper

(You'll need a Bible.)

Tell the kids that a long time ago when Jesus lived, there was a big "difference" that separated people from each other. It was leprosy. No one would go near someone with leprosy. In fact, once you got the disease you were forced out of the city and had to live in caves or other places, surrounded only by people who also had leprosy. You were cut off from your family forever.

Tell the kids they're going to act out a story about Jesus and the leper. Toss a coin. If it's heads, the circles are the leprosy group; if it's tails, the triangles are the leprosy group.

Tell the leprosy kids to go to one side of the room, and tell the other group to avoid them.

Pick up the Bible, as you play the part of Jesus. Stand in the center of the room between the two groups and read aloud Luke 5:12. Ask the lepers to repeat the words "Lord, heal me." Then motion for them to come to you and get on their knees around you.

Read aloud Luke 5:13: "I want to. Be healed."

Whisper to the lepers (so the other group can't hear) to take off their sacks, pile them beside you and come sit down around you.

Invite the other group to come and join you if they can figure out what they have to do first. (The secret is for them to take off their sacks and put them in the pile also.) You may need to whisper this to one of the other group to start the process.

4. Different or the Same?

Sit in a circle together and discuss:

- **What are you thinking or feeling right now?**
- **Who was the better group? Why?**
- **What did you learn about Jesus in this story?**
- **What did you learn about differences from this experience?**

Say: **With Jesus, there are no differences. Jesus loves the people with leprosy as much as he loves all of us. He loves the circles and he loves the triangles. He loves everyone. No group is ignored. All people are accepted.**

5. It's Okay to Be Different

(Place a piece of newsprint on the floor. You'll also need crayons.)

Gather the kids around the newsprint. Ask kids to trace their hands on the paper using the crayons.

Say: **We've discovered that it's tough being different. Here are all our hand prints. Every one of them is different. Every one of us is different. But God still loves us. Think of ways people are different from you that make you not want to be around them. I'll write each difference in one of the hand prints.**

Kids might say differences such as "People who are mean" or "People who don't take care of themselves." Fill up the collage of hand prints.

Ask children how they think God wants us to act toward people who are different from us. After you hear a variety of answers, read some good advice found in 1 Samuel 16:7, "God does not see the same way people see. People look at the outside of a person, but the Lord looks at the heart."

Ask kids to discuss what it means that God looks at a person's heart. After some discussion, say: **We can be different for many reasons. But God knows if we care about others and love them.**

6. Hurting Others

(You'll need paper, a pencil and a trash can.)

Ask children to think of ways we hurt others who seem different from us. For example, talk about them behind their back, laugh at them, don't include them in our games. Write each thing they say on a separate piece of paper, crumple it and put it in a pile.

After you've made a considerable pile, give kids each one or more and let them throw the crumpled papers at group members. Call time, then ask:

- **How did it feel to have others throw papers at you?**
- **How did it feel to throw papers at others?**
- **What would it feel like if the papers were rocks?**
- **How do we hurt others with our words and actions?**

Have kids take each wad and throw it in the trash can as a symbol of trying not to hurt others.

7. Accepting Others

Ask the kids to go back to the pile of sacks and find theirs. Without saying who they're thinking of, have each think of one person who is different for some reason. The person may be new at school, speak another language or be from another country. Ask kids to get to know the person better.

Tell kids to take home the sack that they traded for and keep it in their room. Encourage kids to remember to be more accepting of people who are different from them.

8. Snack in a Sack

(You'll need a sack filled with a variety of fruit or candy for each person.)

Give kids each a snack in a sack. Call attention to the variety of sizes and colors, but point out that they all taste good! Say: **Just like the candy is different, we're all different. But we're all God's children. God loves us all the same.**

When kids finish their snack, close with a prayer thanking God for the variety of people he has created.

by Mike Gillespie

Part 3: A Lively Look at My Faith

Who Is God?

Children this age know that God loves them and cares for them. They enjoy talking about God and praying to him. One difficult concept to teach children is that God exists as three persons—God the Father, God the Son and God the Holy Spirit.

Use this lesson to help children understand who God is and to show them how much God cares for them.

A POWERFUL PURPOSE

Children will learn about God as Father, Son and Holy Spirit. They'll learn about his love for them.

A LOOK AT THE LESSON

1. What Does God Look Like? (8 minutes)
2. God as Father (7 minutes)
3. God as Son (5 minutes)
4. God as Holy Spirit (5 minutes)
5. Three in One (5 minutes)
6. God Triangle (5 minutes)
7. All Three on Our Side (5 minutes)

A SPRINKLING OF SUPPLIES

Gather glue; paper; crayons; a chalkboard and chalk; an egg; a bowl; a Bible; red, blue and yellow construction paper; and cookies containing chocolate chips, butterscotch chips and M&M's.

THE LIVELY LESSON

1. What Does God Look Like?

(You'll need paper and crayons.)

As children arrive, give them each blank paper and crayons. Tell kids each to draw a picture of God. After a few minutes, have kids show and explain their drawings. Then say: **We really don't know what God looks like. But we can learn a lot about him from what the Bible tells us. Today we're going to see who God is and look at some of the things he does for us.**

2. God as Father

(Write Romans 8:28 on a chalkboard: "We know that in everything God works for the good of those who love him.")

Gather the children by the chalkboard, then say: **One thing we know from the Bible is that God is like a father to us. Only he's better than the very best father who ever lived. In Romans 8:28, we read that God works for the good of those who love him. He takes care of us better than any earthly father could.**

Be sensitive to kids who aren't living with their fathers. You might want to point out that God can help us like a father especially when we don't have a father at home.

Let kids each turn to a person sitting close by them. Ask the pairs to think of one or two things the very best father might do for his children. For example, wipe their tears, hug them, fix their bike, fly a kite. Then have the pairs get up and act out one thing a good father might do for his children.

Let the others try to guess.

If no one guesses within 30 seconds, have the actors reveal their actions. After each action ask, **How might God do something like this for us?** For example, God gives us friends to play with, he cares for us when we're sad.

When kids are finished ask, **How did you feel getting up to act out something for the class?**

Say: **When you acted up front, it took time for others to figure out what you were doing. Some kids may have laughed. But you each did your good actions anyway. God is like that. Even when we don't realize what he's doing, God continues to do good things for us. And he loves us more than the best earthly father ever could.**

3. God as Son

(You'll need a Bible, paper and crayons.)

Hand out another blank sheet of paper. Say: **Another thing we learn from the Bible is that God is also Jesus. What does the Bible tell us about Jesus?**

Let kids each respond. Then tell them God loved us so much that he sent his son to us. Jesus died for us so that we will live forever.

Invite the children to draw pictures of Jesus. As kids are drawing read John 3:16 from a children's Bible, or read this version: "For God loved the world so much that he gave his only Son. God gave his Son so that whoever believes in him may not be lost, but have eternal life."

After the artists finish drawing, let them describe their pictures. How is their Jesus drawing different from their God drawing? the same? When all kids have shown their drawings, sing "Jesus Loves Me" together.

4. God as Holy Spirit

(You'll need cookies made with three goodies: chocolate chips, butterscotch chips and M&M's. Use a chocolate chip cookie recipe, but add the other ingredients also.)

Ask, **Is anybody hungry?**

After the cheers die down, give kids the cookies. Be sure they have enough to make a difference in their hunger level. Point out that each cookie contains three ingredients—chocolate chips, butterscotch chips and M&M's. Three parts, but one cookie. Just like God is one God, but three persons—Father, Son and Holy Spirit.

Munch awhile, then ask: **Do your tummies feel any different now than they did before you ate your snack? Why?**

Allow time for discussion, then say: **Even though we don't look any different and no one can see the snack we ate, we feel different, don't we? It's like that when we have God's spirit, the Holy Spirit, living in us. No one can see him, but we know we're different. He lives in us and helps us do what's right. And he is God, just like God is the Father and Jesus.**

5. Three in One

(You'll need an egg and a bowl.)

Say: **It's kind of hard to understand that God is the Father and Jesus and the Holy Spirit—and that he's one at the same time, isn't it? Here's something that might help us understand God a bit better.**

Hold up an egg. Ask, **What is this?** Then break the egg into a bowl without breaking the yolk of the egg. Lay the egg shell in the bowl beside it.

Ask, **Is this still an egg?**

Hold up the shell and ask, **What is this?**

One at a time, point at the egg white and yolk, and ask kids, **What is this?**

Then ask, **But didn't you say all this was an egg?**

Say: **This egg being three parts is a little bit like God being three persons. The three are different, but they're all egg. God's three persons are different, but they're all God.**

6. God Triangle

(Cut out 8×2 strips of red, yellow and blue construction paper. On the red strips write "Father," on the yellow strips write "Jesus," on the blue strips write "Holy Spirit." Make an example to show the kids by gluing three different-color strips in the shape of a triangle as shown in the "Trinity Triangle" diagram.)

Give the kids each a red, yellow and blue strip of construction paper. Have them glue their strips to form a triangle. Show them your example.

Ask them to turn their triangle so one corner points up. Ask them to write a "G" on the top point, an "O" on the lower left point, and a "D" on the lower right point. Show them how the letters spell "God." (You do it first so they see how it should be done.)

Say: **This triangle can help us remember a little bit about God: He's our Heavenly Father, he's Jesus, and he's the Holy Spirit—all at the same time.**

7. All Three on Our Side

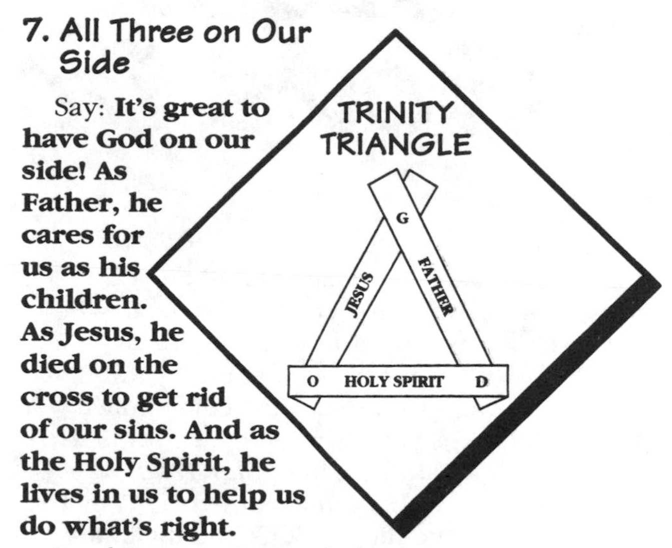

Say: **It's great to have God on our side! As Father, he cares for us as his children. As Jesus, he died on the cross to get rid of our sins. And as the Holy Spirit, he lives in us to help us do what's right.**

Read Romans 8:28 to kids again: "We know that in everything God works for the good of those who love him." Memorize the verse by using these actions.

We know (Point to head)

That in everything (Motion hands all around)

God (Point up)

Works (Pretend to hammer a nail)

For the good of those (Point toward everyone in the room)

Who love (Hug yourself)

Him (Point up)

If you want, let your class develop different actions to the verse. Say: **Today we've seen ways God takes care of us as our heavenly Father, as Jesus, and as the Holy Spirit. And we can trust him to help us just like he tells us he will.**

Encourage kids to take their triangles home as a reminder that God is three persons and he works for the good of those who love him.

by Paul Woods

JESUS—GOD'S SON

Can you remember when you were in elementary school? Who was your favorite hero? Maybe it was Superman, who could fly through the air faster than a speeding bullet. Perhaps your hero was a TV star such as Captain Kirk from *Star Trek*.

Many children have heroes. They try to imitate their actions and their attitudes. We get concerned, however, when children begin to imitate heroes who don't promote Christlike behavior and attitudes.

Use this lesson to show children the ultimate hero: Jesus.

A POWERFUL PURPOSE

Children will learn about Jesus and his power.

A LOOK AT THE LESSON

1. I Need Help (7 minutes)
2. Help From a Friend (4 minutes)
3. Break Into Show Biz (8 minutes)
4. Jesus' Power (5 minutes)
5. Watercolor Painting (8 minutes)
6. Super Snacks (6 minutes)
7. More Help (3 minutes)
8. Memory Time (4 minutes)

A SPRINKLING OF SUPPLIES

Gather a Bible, chairs, flashlights, white construction paper, watercolor paints, paintbrushes, old shirts or aprons, newspaper, sandwiches, napkins, juice, cups, and a table or plastic swimming pool.

THE LIVELY LESSON

1. I Need Help

As children arrive, greet them and tell them how glad you are to see them. Ask them to sit on the floor. Say: **Let's try an experiment. I want you to stand up without using your hands or arms. You can't cross your legs or get on your knees to get up either. Can you do it?**

After several attempts, ask kids each to sit on the floor back-to-back to another person. Have them interlock both arms at the elbows. Say: **Now try standing up. Again, you can't touch the floor with your hands, arms or knees. But you can lean against your partner and work up to a standing position.** Now all kids should be able to stand up—with a little help from a friend.

2. Help From a Friend

Gather in a circle and discuss:

- **Why was it difficult to get up on your own?**
- **How was it easier when you had a partner to help you?**

Say: **Your partner supported you. Your partner gave you power to stand up. If one person, like your partner, can help you do something like this, think of what power Jesus, the Son of God, could give you to do hard things. Jesus is a great hero because he gives us power to do great things.**

Ask children what areas they need help with. For example, doing well in school, not being jealous of others, not fighting with a brother or sister.

Say: **Jesus helps us do these difficult things. Jesus is a real hero because he loves us.**

3. Break Into Show Biz

(You'll need a Bible, three flashlights, chairs, and a table or a child's plastic swimming pool.)

Tell kids they're about to break into show biz and produce a Bible story. Assign the following jobs according to the number of participants in your group:

- Several children to be disciples in the boat. They can sit on the table or sit in the swimming pool, depending on which item you're using as the boat. If you have a lot of kids, set up more tables so you have plenty of room in the boat.
- Someone to be Jesus. Position Jesus on the opposite side of the room.
- Someone to be Peter. Peter starts out in the boat.
- Two kids to film the production. (Pantomime holding a camera.) Position them on either side of the boat.
- Three kids to be light people. Hand each a flashlight. Position two on chairs and one on the floor. Have them shine their lights on the action.

Tell them to listen as you read about Peter walking on the water (Matthew 14:22-33). Direct the action as you go:

Lights! (Lights people give a thumbs-up sign.)

Cameras! (Camera people give a thumbs-up sign.)

Action! (All actors give a thumbs-up sign.)

All the disciples were in a boat. (Disciples sway back and forth.)

It was a stormy night. (Really sway back and forth.)

They were scared. (Disciples chew on fingernails, cower, look frightened.)

They saw Jesus walking to them across the water. (Disciples point, look surprised. Jesus begins walking.)

They were scared. (Disciples chew on fingernails, cower, look frightened.)

Peter yelled, "Lord! If it's you, tell me to come to you on the water." (Peter yells, hands cupped around his mouth to be heard over the storm.)

Jesus replied, "Come." (Jesus says "Come," and motions for Peter to join him.)

Peter started out of the boat; he kept his eyes on Jesus. (Peter begins.)

He took a few steps. (Peter walks.)

He took a few more steps. (And walks.)

Then he got afraid and looked at the water, not at Jesus. (Peter takes his eyes off Jesus and looks at the water.)

He started to sink. (Peter pretends to sink, holding up his hand.)

Jesus reached out to Peter. (Jesus takes Peter's hand.)

They climbed into the boat. (Jesus helps Peter into the boat.)

The wind and the storm stopped. Everyone was amazed. (Disciples place hands over their mouths, wide-eyed, look at Jesus.)

They worshiped Jesus. (Disciples bow their heads and fold their hands.)

They all said, "You are the Son of God." (All disciples say the words with feeling.)

If you want, you could actually videotape the story, then play it back for kids to reinforce the point.

4. Jesus' Power

Say: **Cut! It's a take! Lights off. Cameras off. Actors take a break. Join me in a circle.**

Ask:

● **Who gave Peter the power to walk on water?**

● **What happened when Peter took his eyes off Jesus?**

Say: **Peter sank when he did not trust Jesus to help him walk on the stormy water. We need to trust Jesus when things don't go well. Jesus is a real hero because he has the power to help us out of the stormiest, worst situations we might ever face.**

5. Watercolor Painting

(You'll need white construction paper, paintbrushes, watercolor paints, old shirts or aprons. Spread newspapers in the painting area.)

Tell kids they're going to use watercolors to paint their favorite scene from that watery, stormy production about Jesus and Peter. For example, they could paint the disciples rocking in the storm-tossed boat, or they could paint Jesus reaching out to Peter.

Lead children to the supplies. Cover their good clothes with old shirts or aprons. Let them paint whatever they want.

As the pictures dry, move on to the snack time.

6. Super Snacks

(You'll need sandwiches, juice, cups and napkins.)

Serve the super snacks to the wonderful kids. Ask them if there's anything we ever eat or drink that reminds us of Jesus.

Say: **When we participate in communion, or the Lord's Supper, we think about Jesus. It reminds us that he died for us and rose again. Jesus promises we'll live forever with him in heaven.**

7. More Help

While kids finish eating, remind them of the discussion from activity 2. Give them time to think of more areas in which they need help. Ideas could be:

● Becoming happy again when you're sad.

● Telling the truth when you know you've been wrong.

● Not being afraid when you're alone.

8. Memory Time

Read Philippians 4:13: "I can do all things through Christ because he gives me strength."

Have kids repeat it several times.

Say: **I'm going to mention each thing we've talked about—things we need help with. After each one, point to yourself and say "I can do all things," then point up and say "through Christ because he gives me strength."**

After you mention each of them, have all kids shout: "Thank you, Jesus! Amen!"

Let children take home their watercolor paintings. Or, hang them on a church bulletin board under a title "Jesus Helps Us Through Stormy Times."

by Ray and Cindy Peppers

All Tied Up in Sin

Sin is no easy topic. Yet sin is a crucial issue in Christianity. It's what separates us from God. It's the reason Jesus died. Use this lesson to teach children about sin and about God's great gift of forgiveness.

A POWERFUL PURPOSE

Children will learn about sin and forgiveness.

A LOOK AT THE LESSON

1. Balloon Burst (6 minutes)
2. Sin Slips (6 minutes)
3. Concentration on Sin (8 minutes)
4. Card Conversation (7 minutes)
5. All Tied Up (8 minutes)
6. How Dark Is Sin? (5 minutes)
7. "Initial" Response (5 minutes)

A SPRINKLING OF SUPPLIES

Gather a Bible, balloons, a pencil, slips of paper, photocopies of handouts, yarn or clothesline, Kool-Aid, cookies, food coloring, a spoon, cups and napkins.

THE LIVELY LESSON

1. Balloon Burst

(You'll need balloons, a pencil and slips of paper. On each slip, write a sin such as lying, stealing, hating, and saying bad things about others. Roll the "sin slips" of paper and stuff one sin in each balloon. Inflate the balloons and tie them. Prepare one balloon for each child.)

As children arrive, give them each a balloon. Divide into two teams and line them up on one side of the room.

Go to the other side and say: **We're going to play a relay called "Balloon Burst." On "Go," the first person in each line must run across the room to me, sit on his or her balloon until it bursts, runs back to the line, and tag the next person, who does the same. The first team to burst all its balloons wins. Ready? Any questions? Go!**

2. Sin Slips

(You'll need the slips of paper.)

After the teams burst all their balloons, ask some kids to help you gather the slips of paper. The other kids gather the broken balloons and throw them away. Gather in a circle and read the "sin slips." Ask:

- **What do each of these words have in common?**
- **Have you ever done any of them? If so, which ones?**
- **What does the word "sin" mean?**

Say: **Sin is when we do something that's wrong. We all sin. We've all done something written on these slips of paper. Let's hear what the Bible says about sin.**

Read aloud Romans 3:23: **"For all have sinned and fall short of the glory of God."** (NIV)

Say: **Everyone has sinned or done wrong in God's eyes. But the good news is that Jesus saves us. God forgives us. Let's learn a little more about sin.**

3. Concentration on Sin

(You'll need two photocopies of the "Love God" handout and two photocopies of the "Hate Sin" handout. Cut apart the squares and shuffle them.)

Ask children to sit in a circle. Inside the circle, place the cards face down randomly. Say: **Each of these cards has an identical match. We're going to find all the matches. I'll start first, so you can see how it's done. Then we'll go around the circle. The first person must turn over two cards and see if they say the same thing. I'll read them for you. If they match, the person keeps the pair of cards and goes again. If they don't match, thc person turns the cards face down and the next person gets to choose.**

Play until all cards are matched. Read aloud the verses on the card and talk about what they say about sin.

4. Card Conversation

(You'll need a Bible and one set of the cards taped to the wall so the first letters of the words spell "Love God" and "Hate sin" vertically. Photocopy more "Love God" and "Hate Sin" handouts. Cut apart the cards and shuffle them. Make enough so each person has a set.)

Point to the letters and tell kids that they spell "Love God; hate sin." The "Love God" cards tell how to draw closer to God. Ask, **How does someone who loves God act?** Read the cards and the Bible verses. The Bible verses help explain the more difficult words such as "victorious," "generous" and "disciplined."

The "Hate Sin" cards tell more about sins. Ask, **What are some of the sins listed on the cards?** Read the cards and the Bible verses. The Bible verses help explain the more difficult words such as "envy" and "idolatry."

Give kids each two sets of the "Love God" and "Hate Sin" cards. Tell children to take the cards home and play the matching game from activity 3. Encourage kids to ask parents or brothers and sisters to help look up the Bible verses and read them.

5. All Tied Up

(You'll need yarn or clothesline.)

Ask children to regroup in their two relay teams. Instruct them each to pair off within their teams and stand back to back, arms at their sides. Tie each pair together around the waist with yarn or clothesline.

Say: **This relay lets you feel how hard it is to be "tied up" by sin. On the word "go," the first pair in both teams runs up to me and back to the line, then the next pairs run. First team to finish wins.**

Run the relay. Afterward ask:

- **How did it feel to be "all tied up" in sin?**
- **What was hardest about it?**
- **How is this game like times you've done something wrong?**

6. How Dark Is Sin?

(You'll need Kool-Aid, cookies, a see-through glass, four colors of food coloring, a spoon, small cups and napkins.)

Pour several small cups of Kool-Aid and ask for volunteers to drink.

LOVE GOD

Photocopy this handout. Cut the cards apart and shuffle them.

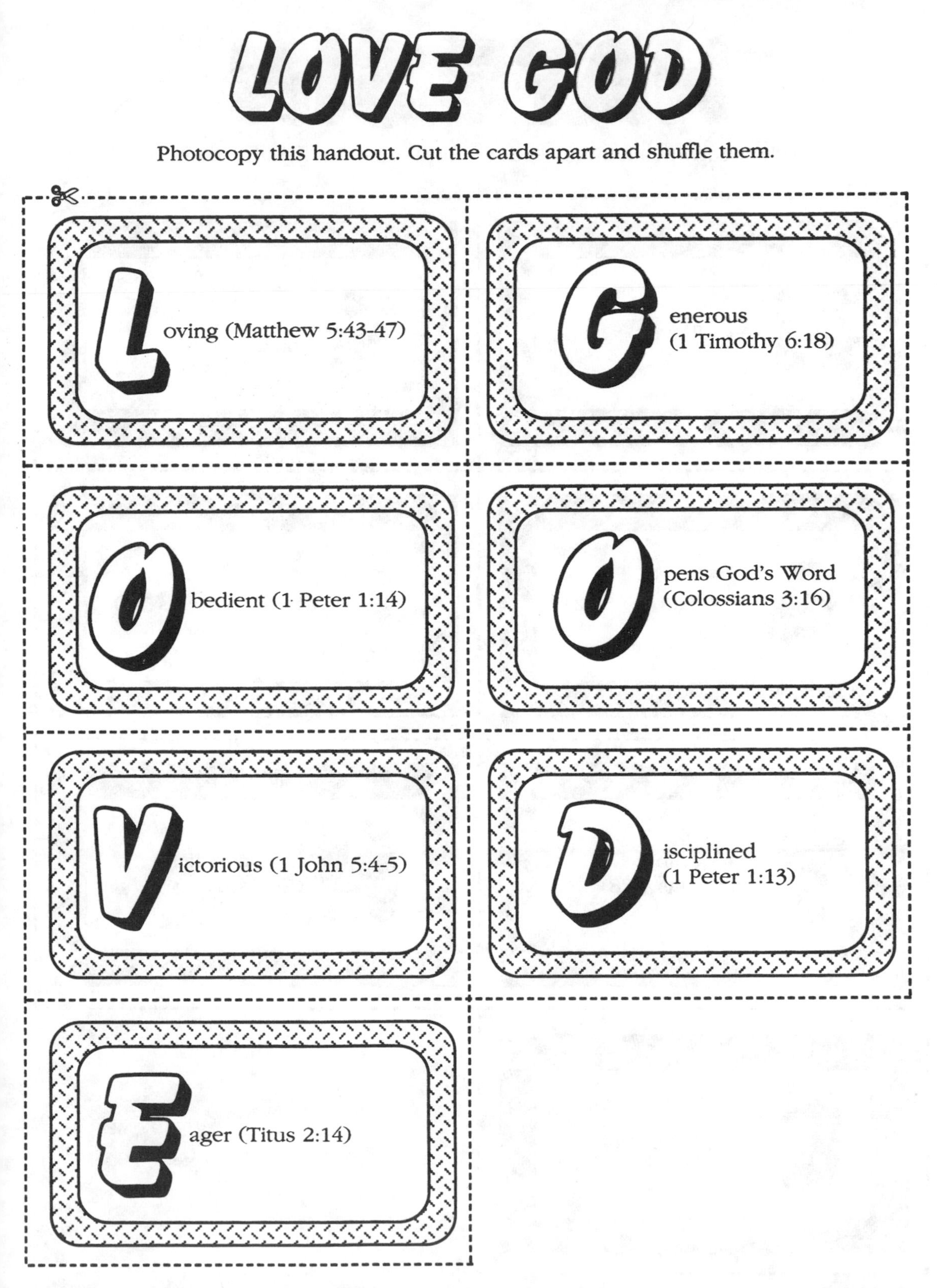

Permission to photocopy this handout granted for local church use. Copyright © Group Books, Box 481, Loveland, CO 80539.

HATE SIN

Photocopy this handout. Cut the cards apart and shuffle them.

Permission to photocopy this handout granted for local church use. Copyright © Group Books, Box 481, Loveland, CO 80539.

Choose a child to sample the Kool-Aid and sit down.

Then add a few drops of food coloring, any color, to each remaining cup. Repeat your request for a volunteer to sample the drink. Volunteers will realize that the food coloring really doesn't change the taste. It just looks strange. Keep repeating this process until the Kool-Aid looks muddy brown and you can no longer get a volunteer to sample it.

Compare the muddy-color Kool-Aid to sin. Say: **When we first added food coloring to the drink, it didn't look so bad. But we kept adding it until it looked terrible. This is like sin. One sin may not look so bad. However, the more sin in a person's life, the more mixed up and sad the person. God wants us clean. He forgives us.**

Hold up the "clean" Kool-Aid. Pour cups for the kids and pass out cookies. Eat and enjoy the clear, clean taste of forgiveness.

7. "Initial" Response

(You'll need photocopies of the "ABC's of Reasons Not to Sin" handout.)

Form a circle and let kids continue eating their snack while you read the "ABC's of Reasons Not to Sin" handout. One at a time, take the first initial of a person's name, then read the corresponding sentence. For example, Karen's first initial is K, the K reason for not sinning is "You are a child of the King."

Do this for each person in the circle. Give kids each a copy of the handout to take home and show their family members.

Close by reading 1 John 1:9. Say: **Remember. Even if you do the wrong thing, Jesus loves you. Tell him you're sorry. He'll forgive you.**

by Patti Chromey

ABC's OF REASONS NOT TO SIN

A—God **ADOPTED** you as his child.

B—You **BELONG** to God.

C—You were **CHOSEN** by God.

D—Jesus **DIED** for you.

E—God gives you **ETERNAL** life.

F—God is your **FATHER**.

G—**GOD** loves you.

H—**HEAVEN** will be your home.

I—You were made in God's **IMAGE**.

J—**JESUS** helps you not sin.

K—You are a child of the **KING**.

L—God **LOVES** you so much, he doesn't want you to sin.

M—You are a **MIRACLE**, you are special.

N—God calls you by **NAME**, you are his own.

O—**OBEY** God because he loves you.

P—Everything is **POSSIBLE** with God's help.

Q—You are God's **QUALITY** creation.

R—Heaven is your **REWARD**.

S—God **SELECTED** you to be his child.

T—**TRUST** God to help you.

U—God **UNDERSTANDS** that it's hard to do the right thing.

V—God will give you **VICTORY** over sin.

W—God said you'll **WIN** if you follow him.

X—You are an **X-CELLENT** creation.

Y—God **YEARNS**, or really wants you to follow him.

Z—God wants you to be **ZEALOUS**, or enthusiastic, in doing right.

Permission to photocopy this handout granted for local church use. Copyright © Group Books, Box 481, Loveland, CO 80539.

Heaven Is a Wonderful Place

"Heaven is a wonderful place!" These words to a children's song are more than sentiment. Heaven *is* a wonderful place. A place of hope. A place of security. A place of life. A place of love. Use this lesson to help children discover the incredible wonders and fun of heaven.

A POWERFUL PURPOSE

Children will learn about that wonderful place: heaven.

A LOOK AT THE LESSON

1. Heaven Hunt (5 minutes)
2. Heavenly Collage (8 minutes)
3. Dreamy Discussion (4 minutes)
4. The Bible Says (4 minutes)
5. Heavenly Hugs (7 minutes)
6. Heavenly Snack (6 minutes)
7. Hear a Cheer (4 minutes)

A SPRINKLING OF SUPPLIES

Gather construction paper, 3×5 cards, glue, scissors, magazines, catalogs, a Bible, masking tape, angel food cake or some other heavenly snack.

THE LIVELY LESSON

1. Heaven Hunt

(You'll need 3×5 cards. Write each of the following words on a separate card: "Heaven is a wonderful place." Hide the cards around the room before class.)

When children arrive, say: **Today we're going to discover new things about heaven. I have hidden five cards around the room. Let's all work together to find the cards, and then figure out what they say.**

When children have figured out the sentence, ask:

- **What was it like to look for cards when you didn't know what they said?**
- **How did it feel when you found a card?**
- **How did it feel when we figured out what the cards said together?**

Say: **Just as we had fun finding this sentence, we're going to have fun today finding out about heaven.**

2. Heavenly Collage

(You'll need several old magazines, catalogs, scissors, glue and construction paper.)

Give children construction paper, glue, scissors, magazines and catalogs. Instruct them each to cut out pictures that best describe heaven as they understand it, then paste them onto the construction paper any way they want so that each child has a collage.

3. Dreamy Discussion

(You'll need masking tape.)

As the children finish, talk to them about their collages. Let them describe their thoughts about heaven. Ask:

● **If you were to dream about heaven, what would it look like?**

● **How would you feel in heaven?**

● **Who would live in heaven?**

Hang the collages with masking tape where kids can see them during the rest of the lesson.

4. The Bible Says

(You'll need a Bible.)

Say: **We've seen some of your ideas about heaven shown in your "Heavenly Collage." We've heard some of your ideas in our "Dreamy Discussion." Now let's hear some heavenly descriptions from the Bible.**

Read these verses, or use a favorite children's Bible translation. After each verse you read, have kids stand and say: "Heaven is a wonderful place!" then sit back down.

● **"The Lord has set his throne in heaven. And his kingdom rules over everything"** (Psalm 103:19).

● **"You should be happy because your names are written in heaven** (Luke 10:20b).

● **"And God will wipe away every tear from their eyes"** (Revelation 7:17).

● **"Each gate was made from a single pearl. The street of the city was made of pure gold. The gold was clear as glass"** (Revelation 21:21).

5. Heavenly Hugs

Say: **The Bible tells us some things about heaven, but no one really knows exactly what it's like. The main thing we do know is that heaven is a wonderful, fun place, filled with love—because God is love.**

Tell kids that you're going to call out numbers, and kids are supposed to quickly form groups that size and do a big group hug. If the group doesn't evenly divide into the number you call, the extra kids can join in with another group for the hug. Also, kids can't be beside the same person twice in a row. As leader, participate in the hugging too.

Call out various numbers, and make sure all kids are included in the hug. For the final number, say the number of your whole group's size, have a giant hug, sit down, then ask these questions:

● **What was most fun about the activity?**

● **How did it feel to be hugged by a lot of different people?**

● **How would you like to be in a place where everyone loves everyone else?**

Explain that being in heaven will be fun and wonderful because everyone loves everyone. Allow time for children to ask further questions about heaven. Don't be afraid to say "I don't know" in response. Let kids know that no one except God knows exactly what heaven will be like.

6. Heavenly Snack

(You'll need angel food cake or some other heavenly snack.)

Serve the snacks. Let kids munch as they wander through the "art gallery" of their collages of heaven.

7. Hear a Cheer

Teach the following cheer, adapted from the song "Heaven Is a Wonderful Place." You say one line, and kids repeat it. Get louder as you go until you shout the last line.

Heaven is
A wonderful place
Warm, bright
Filled with grace
I want to go there
One of these days
Heaven is a wonderful place
Amen!

Take down the collages, and let kids take them home as reminders.

by Patti Chromey

Part 4: A Lively Look at Celebrations

Birthday Bash

Birthdays are important to children. Kids enjoy the celebration and look forward to that special day. They also enjoy being part of a friend's birthday celebration. Use this lesson to remind children that God created and loves each one of them. They're all special!

A POWERFUL PURPOSE

Children will celebrate the joy of birthdays.

A LOOK AT THE LESSON

1. Custom Invitations (5 minutes)
2. Musical Invitations (3 minutes)
3. Party Hats (7 minutes)
4. How Do You Celebrate? (3 minutes)
5. A Star Was Born (5 minutes)
6. My Birthday Cake (7 minutes)
7. Personal Presents (6 minutes)
8. A Present From God (4 minutes)
9. Happy Birthday Snack (5 minutes)

A SPRINKLING OF SUPPLIES

Gather posterboard, staples and stapler, crayons, upbeat music, elastic string, paper plates, construction paper, glue, scissors, tape, ribbon, birthday cake, candles, napkins, cups, forks, drinks, a Bible, yarn, hole punch and photocopies of the handout. An instant-print camera and film are optional.

THE LIVELY LESSON

1. Custom Invitations

(You'll need construction paper, crayons and scissors.)

As children arrive, explain that today you're celebrating everyone's birthday, and you want them each to make an invitation to invite a friend in the class to the party. Give children each a folded piece of construction paper, and let them design invitations. Have them each write their own name on the invitation.

2. Musical Invitations

(You'll need invitations from activity 1 and upbeat music.)

When kids are ready, have them sit in a circle, holding their invitations. Say: **Now we're going to invite each other to the party! When I turn on the music, pass your card to your friend on the right. Continue passing the card as long as the music plays. As soon as the music stops, look to see who's invitation you're holding, then race to sit in that person's seat.** Play music several times, giving kids time to move around a lot.

3. Party Hats

(You'll need posterboard, elastic and crayons. You'll also need a stapler.)

Say: **Now that everyone has been invited to the party, we need to**

make party hats. Have kids go to the party hat table. Ask kids to pretend they're getting ready for a birthday party at their house. Have kids each decorate a piece of posterboard with crayons. Then staple each board into a cone-shape party hat. Attach elastic for a chin strap. Have them wear their hats for the rest of the lesson.

4. How Do You Celebrate?

(You'll need the completed birthday hats.)

Gather in a circle. Ask each child to describe something special about his or her hat. Ask:

- **Why are birthdays so important to you?**
- **Whose birthdays do you celebrate at your house?**

Say: **Let's always remember that God made us. We should always thank God when we have a birthday. Here's what the Bible says about birthdays.**

Read aloud Psalm 139:13-14 from a children's Bible, or read this version: **"You made my whole being. You formed me in my mother's body. I praise you because you made me in an amazing and wonderful way. What you have done is wonderful. I know this very well."**

Say: **We were important, amazing and wonderful to God even before we were born. God made us all special. Just like you made each of the hats special. God loves us very much.**

5. A Star Was Born

(You'll need the "A Star Was Born" handout, crayons, glue, 20-inch pieces of yarn and a hole punch.)

Give kids each crayons and the "A Star Was Born" handout. Tell kids each that on their birthday, a star was born. Have kids draw their own pictures inside the stars. Cut out the star, punch a hole at the top, and string a 20-inch piece of yarn through each one.

Help kids put on their necklaces. As you do, say: **I'm glad you were born, (name). You're a star.**

(If you choose, take an instant-print photo of each person instead of having kids draw their own pictures. Help kids each cut out their picture and glue it in the star.)

6. My Birthday Cake

(You'll need paper plates, construction paper, scissors, crayons and glue.)

Show everyone the supplies. Say: **You can't have a birthday party without a cake. Let's design your next birthday cake out of these supplies.**

Design a birthday cake with the kids so they can see how you do it. Let them each decorate a paper plate with the crayons and construction paper. When children finish, gather in a circle and have kids show their cake designs.

7. Personal Presents

(You'll need a box without writing on it for each child. You'll also need crayons, ribbons and tape.)

Say: **We often get and give presents on birthdays. Usually the presents are things we buy. But we can also give people special presents by doing something for them. For example, we can give our parents the present of helping to set the table or cleaning our rooms.**

Give kids each a box, and have

A STAR WAS BORN

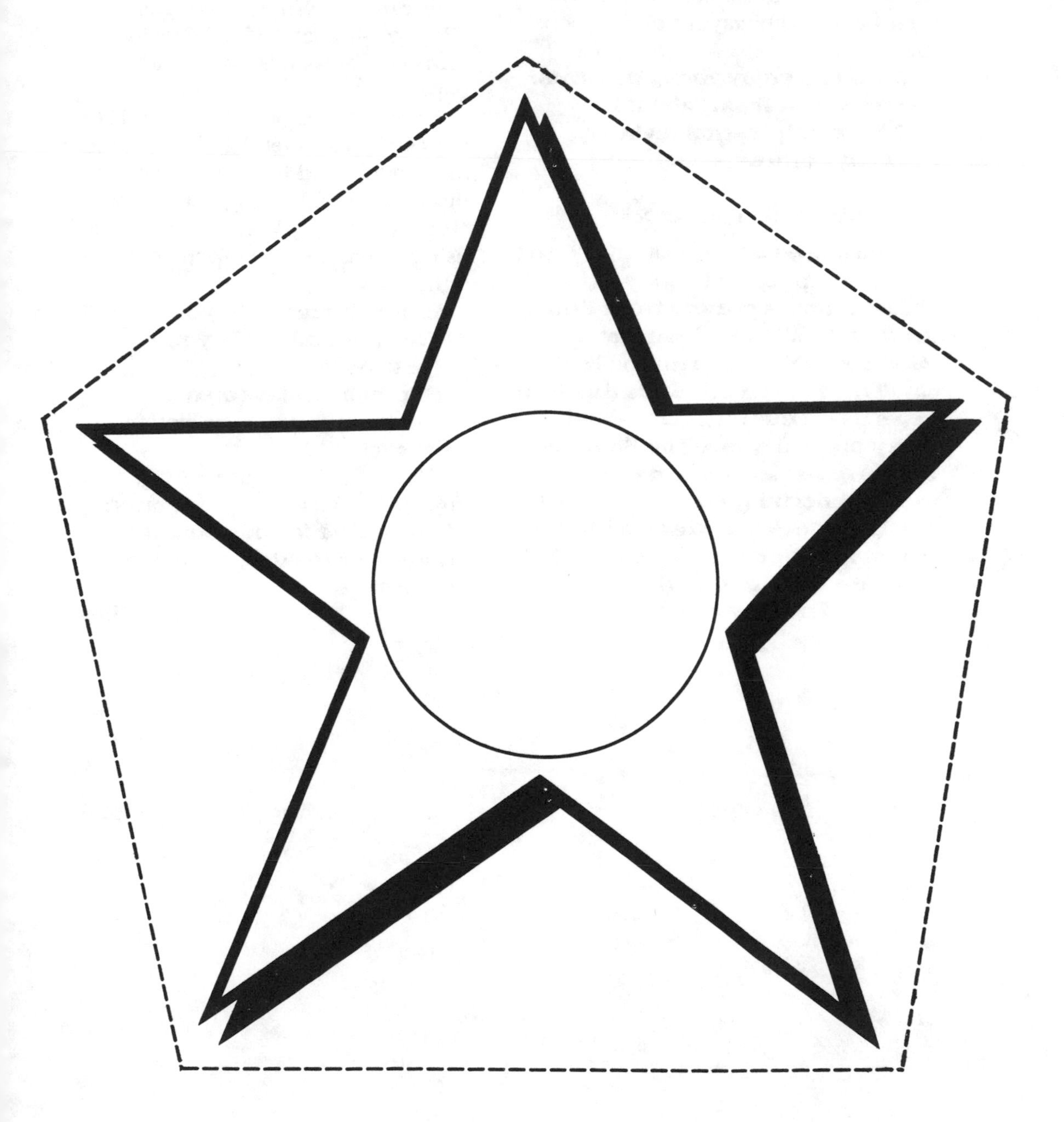

Permission to photocopy this handout granted for local church use.
Copyright © Group Books, Box 481, Loveland, CO 80539.

them decorate their boxes to represent something they want to give as a present to their parents. Let them decorate their boxes with crayons and ribbons. Ask:

● **Do you enjoy giving presents? What's the best part about it?**

● **How do presents make birthdays more special?**

8. A Present From God

(You'll need a heart that says "God Loves Me" for each child.)

Say: **I have a present from God for you, too.** Tape a heart that says "God Loves You" on each child's shirt. Say: **This heart reminds us that God loves us on our birthdays—and every other day too. The Bible says God loves us so much that he gave us a wonderful present: Jesus.** Ask:

● **How does knowing God loves you make your birthday special?**

● **How does getting this present from God make you feel?**

9. Happy Birthday Snack

(You'll need a real birthday cake with candles. Write on the cake "Happy Birthday to Us." Provide drinks, cups, plates, forks and napkins.)

Bring out the birthday cake. Light the candles and let the children blow them out. Stand in a circle and teach the class the following version of "Happy Birthday," with children each using the name of the person on their right.

Happy birthday to you.
I'm glad God made you.
He loves you, dear ____________.
Happy birthday to you.

Eat the cake and refreshments. Celebrate!

When children finish eating, gather in a circle. Close with this prayer: **Thanks, God for our birthdays. Thanks for making us. We love you. Amen.**

by Mike Gillespie

Can You Believe It?

Though we sometimes think children live in an ideal world, reality is quite different. They face serious stresses and problems. They get sad and worried. Easter is an excellent opportunity to show kids that God's love is stronger than the things that make them sad. Use this lesson to show kids that, even when things seem bad, God can work miracles—like he did on Easter morning.

A POWERFUL PURPOSE

Children will learn that God's love is strong enough to raise Jesus from the dead—and to help them deal with problems.

A LOOK AT THE LESSON

1. Knot Untangle (5 minutes)
2. Can It Happen? (4 minutes)
3. Jesus Is Alive! (6 minutes)
4. Looking for Rainbows (6 minutes)
5. What Makes Me Sad (4 minutes)
6. What Makes Me Happy (5 minutes)
7. Is It Really Good? (5 minutes)
8. Sing a Song of Easter (4 minutes)

A SPRINKLING OF SUPPLIES

Gather a pitcher filled with half white vinegar and half water, baking soda, a large bowl, markers, newspaper, construction paper, Bible, crayons, pennies, a clear pitcher of milk with food coloring in it, and cookies.

THE LIVELY LESSON

1. Knot Untangle

When children arrive, have them form circles of no more than five, facing inward. Ask kids to cross their arms and join hands with the people next to them. Then say: **I want you to uncross your arms without letting go of each other's hands and return to a circle with everyone facing inward.**

Give children time to do the activity. When they've finished or have given up, sit together and ask:

- **Did you get frustrated during the activity? Why or why not?**
- **Did you think you'd get untangled? Why or why not?**
- **How did you feel when (if) you got untangled?**

2. Can It Happen?

(You'll need a glass or pitcher filled with half white vinegar and half water. You'll also need some baking soda and a large bowl to catch overflow.)

Hold up the glass or pitcher of water and vinegar, and ask:

- **What do you think it is?**
- **Do you think I can make it fizz up? Why or why not?**

After kids are adequately intrigued, hold the glass or pitcher over the bowl and pour in some baking soda. Watch the fizzing. Ask: **Are you surprised I could do this?**

Say: **Many years ago, something**

happened that people thought was impossible—like many of you thought the fizzing would be impossible. Jesus had died, and all his followers were sad. But then he came to life again. That's why we celebrate Easter.

3. Jesus Is Alive!

(You'll need a construction-paper happy face and sad face for each child. You'll also need a Bible.)

Give children each a happy face and a sad face. Explain that you're going to read the story of Easter from the Bible. Have them hold up their sad faces when the story is sad and their happy faces when the story is happy.

Slowly read John 20:1-18, giving children time to hold up their faces during the story. Afterwards ask:

- **Do you feel happy or sad after hearing this story? Why?**
- **What's the best part of this story?**

4. Looking for Rainbows

(You'll need a sheet of construction paper prepared as follows for every six kids: First, draw a bright rainbow using markers. Then scribble over the entire rainbow with black crayons so you can't see the rainbow any more. You'll also need a penny for each child and newspaper to cover the floor.)

Say: **Sometimes we all feel sad—like the people felt at the beginning of the Bible story.** Have kids mention things that make them sad.

Show kids the black piece of paper. Ask if it looks happy or sad. Then say: **Right now this paper looks dark and sad. But let's see what happens when we scratch off the crayon.**

Cover the floor with newspaper. Have kids form groups of six or fewer and use pennies to scratch off the crayon, revealing the rainbow underneath. When all groups have finished, come together and ask:

- **What did you think you'd find when you started scratching?**
- **How did you feel when you began to see the rainbow?**
- **How is this experience like the way Jesus' followers felt in the Bible story we read?**

5. What Makes Me Sad

(You'll need construction paper and crayons for each child.)

Give children each a sheet of construction paper and some crayons. Ask them to draw something that makes them sad on one side. Have them each explain what they drew. Be sensitive to tough issues they might bring up.

6. What Makes Me Happy

(You'll need the supplies from the previous activity.)

Tell kids to turn over their papers and draw something that makes them happy on the other side. Have them each explain what they drew.

Have kids sit in a circle. Say: **I'm going to read a short story. As I do, hold up your paper to show the right side when I say the word happy or sad.** When kids understand, read the following:

Some things in life make us sad. These things include . . . (mention some of the things on kids' sheets.) **But even when we're sad, God takes care of us and can make us happy. At Easter, Jesus' followers were sad at first. But Jesus rose from the dead, and the disciples were very**

happy! We can be happy, too, because Jesus rose from the dead to save us from our sins.

7. Is It Really *Good?*

(You'll need milk with food coloring in it to make it look unappetizing. You'll also need cookies.)

Hold up a pitcher of the discolored milk and ask:

- **How many of you want to drink this?**
- **What do you think it is?**
- **Do you believe me when I say it tastes good?**

Get a brave child to take the first sample, and convince the whole group to enjoy the milk along with cookies. Say: **Just like some of you didn't believe this milk would taste good, some of Jesus' followers didn't believe the good news that Jesus had risen from the dead. But they were really happy when they learned that he was alive.**

8. Sing a Song of Easter

End the lesson by singing together the following song to the tune of "Row, Row, Row Your Boat." Encourage kids to sing enthusiastically to show how happy they are. If you have time, sing it as a round too.

Hip, hip, hip hurray!
No reason to be sad,
Jesus is alive today.
On Easter, let's be glad!

by Eugene C. Roehlkepartain

THANKS FOR EVERYTHING!

Thanksgiving can be a time to eat turkey and potatoes, watch football and talk about pilgrims. But Thanksgiving also reminds us of God's many good gifts. Use this lesson to help children get past turkeys and football and realize how much they have to be thankful for.

A POWERFUL PURPOSE

Children will thank God for his many gifts.

A LOOK AT THE LESSON

1. A Penny for Your Thanks (5 minutes)
2. Thanks for Everything (7 minutes)
3. Thanksgiving Headband (8 minutes)
4. Thanks, God! (4 minutes)
5. Count Your Popcorn (6 minutes)
6. Offering of Thanks (6 minutes)
7. Add-a-Word Prayer (5 minutes)

A SPRINKLING OF SUPPLIES

Gather pennies, newsprint, markers, crayons, a whistle, scissors, a stapler, photocopies of the "Psalm Thanks" handout, a Bible, popcorn, paper, napkins and an offering plate or basket.

THE LIVELY LESSON

1. A Penny for Your Thanks

(You'll need a penny for each child and an offering plate.)

Welcome children as they arrive. Give them each a penny. Say: **We're going to play a game in which you all try to give away all your pennies to someone else as quickly as possible. You don't want any pennies left. When someone gives you a penny, you must say "thank you" to that person.**

When everyone understands, start the game. After kids have exchanged pennies for a minute or so, stop the game and ask:

- **What was it like to try to give your pennies away?**
- **How did it feel to say thank you so much?**
- **How did it feel to have people thank you for every penny you gave?**

Say: **Today we're talking about Thanksgiving. Just like we had to say thank you a lot in the game, we have lots of reasons to say thank you in real life. And like we enjoyed having people say thank you to us, God likes it when we say thank you to him. Let's put the money in the offering plate to say thank you to God.**

Pass around an offering plate to collect the pennies.

2. Thanks for Everything

(Draw on separate sheets of newsprint a house, a school, a church, and a swing set—to symbolize a playground. See examples in the "Thankful Pictures" diagram. You'll need several of four different colors of crayons. You'll also need a whistle.)

Tape each sheet of newsprint on a different wall. Explain that each sheet represents a different area of life—family, school, church and friends. Give children each a crayon, and have them find the others with the same color. Have each group go to a different sheet.

Explain that they each have one minute to draw something on each sheet that they're thankful for in that area of life. For example, one person might draw food in the house because he or she is thankful for meals with the family. When kids understand, blow the whistle to start the drawing. When a minute's up, blow the whistle again, and have each group race to the next sheet.

When all kids have drawn on all four sheets, take a tour of all the drawings and talk about how much we have to be thankful for. Compliment kids on their great ideas.

3. Thanksgiving Headband

(You'll need scissors, crayons, a stapler and the "Psalm Thanks" handout. If possible, photocopy the handouts on two different colors of paper.)

Give children each a photocopy of the "Psalm Thanks" handout, crayons and scissors. Have them each cut out the leaves, color them and staple them together as a headband. Help them add extra paper so the headbands fit well. Have kids all wear their headbands for the rest of the lesson.

(An option would be to have kids go outside and find leaves in different shapes to trace on construction paper. Then they cut out the shapes and write the verse themselves to make the headbands.)

4. Thanks, God!

(You'll need a Bible.)

Say: **God has given us so many good gifts. And the Bible says we should thank him for them.** Read aloud Psalm 118:1-4. Then say: **This passage talks about Israel and the family of Aaron thanking God for his love. We can also thank God for his love.**

Have kids memorize the line "His love continues forever." Then say the following, and have each group shout this line in response:

Thank the Lord because He is good. His love continues forever. Let the people of this class say ... (The whole class shouts. "His love continues forever.")

Let the boys of this class say ... (Boys say, "His love continues forever.")

Let the girls of this class say ... (Girls say, "His love continues forever.")

Let the people of this class say ... (Everyone says, "His love continues forever.")

Add any variations that are appropriate for your class, such as different ages, teachers or headband color.

5. Count Your Popcorn

(You'll need a cup of popped popcorn and a napkin for each student.)

Give children each a cup of popcorn. Say: **Before we eat our snack, let's count how much we have to be thankful for.** Have kids each dump their popcorn on a napkin and count each piece. Have older kids help younger ones.

When everyone has finished counting, find out how much popcorn different children have. Give more

THANKFUL PICTURES

PSALM THANKS

(Psalm 118:1)

Permission to photocopy this handout granted for local church use. Copyright © Group Books, Box 481, Loveland, CO 80539.

popcorn to those who have less. Then ask:

● **Were you surprised how many pieces of popcorn you had?**

● **Does knowing how much you have make you more thankful? Why or why not?**

Say a short prayer of thanks, then let kids eat their popcorn.

6. Offering of Thanks

(You'll need paper and crayons for each child. You'll also need an offering plate or a basket.)

Say: **When we're thankful for something, we often give something back to the person who gave it to us. For example, if someone gives us a nice present, we may send that person a card. Similarly, when we realize all the good things God gives us, we want to give something back to him. That's why we have offerings in church—as one way of saying thanks to God.**

Give children each a sheet of paper and a crayon. Ask them to draw something they want to give to God as a way of thanking him for all his gifts. They could draw coins to show allowance, a clock to show time, a heart to show love, or a special activity to show service. Help them think of ideas.

When children are ready, say: **Now we'll show that we're giving these things to God by collecting the drawings.** Pass around the offering plate or basket, and have kids put in their drawings. Encourage kids to remember what they gave to God and to do it during the coming week.

If you wish, arrange with your pastor for the drawings to be included in the offering during the worship service.

7. Add-a-Word Prayer

Form a circle and talk more about what kids are thankful for, such as food, friends, family, homes, toys, trees, flowers, pets and animals. Allow each child to choose one thing for which he or she is thankful.

When all kids have thought of something, start out a prayer with these words: **Thank you, God, for ...** Go around the circle and let each child name his or her item. When the last one is added, finish the prayer by saying: **Thank you, God, for all the good things you give us. Thanks most of all for your son, Jesus. Amen.**

by Jolene L. Roehlkepartain

Happy Birthday, Jesus!

Kids love birthday parties. They anticipate the games, the cake, the presents. They generally can't wait for the day of the birthday party!

Christmas is Jesus' birthday. This lesson helps children look forward to and prepare for Christmas with the same anticipation they have for a birthday party. They'll join together in throwing a surprise birthday party for Jesus.

A POWERFUL PURPOSE

Children will celebrate Jesus' birth with a birthday party.

A LOOK AT THE LESSON

1. Surprise! (5 minutes)
2. Party Decorations (8 minutes)
3. The Christmas Story (5 minutes)
4. Christmas Cake Walk (6 minutes)
5. Cake Break (5 minutes)
6. Gifts for Jesus (5 minutes)
7. The Gift of Ourselves (5 minutes)
8. Confetti Cheer (3 minutes)

A SPRINKLING OF SUPPLIES

Gather yarn, upbeat Christmas music, banner-making supplies, red and green crepe paper streamers, scissors, tape, red and green construction paper, red and green balloons, markers, a Bible, birthday cake, juice, plates, napkins, forks, cups, extra toys, a manger or stroller, wrapping paper, flat pans for paint, old shirts, red and green tempera paint, newspaper and supplies for cleaning hands.

THE LIVELY LESSON

1. Surprise!

(You'll need yarn and upbeat music. Make arrangements to use a special classroom for the day.)

Before any kids arrive, wind yarn from your regular classroom to a special, prearranged classroom. Weave it around so kids can't easily tell where the yarn leads. Have other adults or teenagers hide in the classroom to greet the children with "surprise!"

When children arrive, say: **I have a surprise for you today. We have to follow this piece of yarn to find out what the surprise is.** Have kids grab the yarn, then follow it to the special meeting room. When they find the room, have everyone shout "Surprise Party!" and turn on upbeat Christmas music. Ask:

- **What were you expecting when I said I had a surprise today?**
- **What do you like about surprises?**

● **What surprises are there at Christmas?**

Say: **Christmas is filled with surprises: presents, good food, fun. But the best surprise was the surprise of Jesus being born. And that's the real reason we celebrate Christmas.**

2. Party Decorations

(You'll need upbeat Christmas music, banner-making supplies, red and green crepe paper streamers, scissors, tape, construction paper, red and green balloons and markers. Organize the decoration stations as described in the activity.)

Say: **Because Christmas is Jesus' birthday, we're going to have a birthday party for Jesus. To start, we need to decorate the room for a party.**

Form groups to work at the following decoration stations. Have groups rotate until all the decorations are complete. Have an adult supervise at each station. Play music while children decorate. If you have a large group, divide the stations among them and don't rotate.

● **Decoration Station 1—Birthday Banner:** Have these kids make a giant "Happy Birthday, Jesus!" banner on butcher paper or an old sheet. Use supplies such as markers, glitter, swatches of cloth. Leave room for hand prints, as described in activity 7. Hang the banner on the wall.

● **Decoration Station 2—Streamer Stringers:** Using red and green crepe paper streamers, tape and scissors, have the group "deck the room with reams of streamers." Be sure the supervising adult attaches the streamers in high places.

● **Decoration Station 3—Confetti Cutters:** Have this group cut or tear up red and green construction paper to use as confetti. Since this activity won't take as long, have these kids help other teams when they're finished. You'll use the confetti in the closing activity.

● **Decoration Station 4—Balloon Blowers:** Have older kids blow up red and green balloons. Have them write "Happy Birthday, Jesus" with markers, or draw Christmas decorations on them. Then hang the balloons around the room.

When all teams are finished, admire the decorations.

3. The Christmas Story

(You'll need a Bible.)

Say: **We're having this party to celebrate Jesus' birth. That's also the reason we celebrate Christmas. The story of Jesus' birth is told in the Bible. Listen to the story and follow my actions.** Read aloud the following condensed version of Luke 2:1-20, and lead children in the actions described below:

At that time, Augustus Caesar sent an order that all people must list their names in a register (write in the air). **Everyone went to their own towns to be registered.**

So Joseph left Nazareth, a town in Galilee, and went to the town of Bethlehem in Judea (march in place). **Joseph registered with Mary because she was engaged to marry him** (hold hands). **While Joseph and Mary were in Bethlehem, the time came for her to have a baby** (hold arms as if rocking a baby). **She gave birth to her first son. There were no rooms left in the inn** (shake finger "no"). **So she wrapped the baby in cloths** (make wrapping motion)

and laid him in a box (lay imaginary baby down) **where animals are fed** (chew like animals).

That night, some shepherds were in the fields nearby watching their sheep (use hands to make binoculars). **An angel of the Lord stood before them** (stretch arms wide). **The glory of the Lord was shining around them, and suddenly they became very frightened** (act afraid). **The angel said to them, "Don't be afraid, because I am bringing you some good news** (smile). **It will be a joy to all people** (clap). **Today your Savior was born in David's town** (hold arms as if rocking a baby). **He is Christ, the Lord. You will find a baby** (hold arms as if rocking a baby) **wrapped in cloths** (make wrapping motion) **and lying** (lay imaginary baby down) **in a feeding box** (chew like animals).

Then the angels left the shepherds (wave goodbye) **and went back to heaven. The shepherds said to each other, "Let us go to Bethlehem and see this thing that has happened"** (act like you're talking).

So the shepherds went quickly (jog in place) **and found Mary and Joseph. And the shepherds saw the baby** (hold arms as if rocking a baby) **lying in a feeding box** (chew like animals). **Then they told what the angels** (spread arms wide) **said to them. Then the shepherds went back to their sheep, praising God and thanking him for everything that they had seen and heard** (clap and cheer).

After the story, ask:

● **What's most exciting about this story?**

● **How would you have felt if you had been a shepherd? if you had been Mary or Joseph?**

4. Christmas Cake Walk

(You'll need construction paper and a marker.)

Before class, write the answers to these questions (answer in parentheses) on construction paper. Use enough questions so you have one for each child. Make up more questions as needed:

● Whose birthday do we celebrate at Christmas? (Jesus)

● Who was Jesus' mother? (Mary)

● Who told the shepherds about Jesus' birth? (Angels)

● What town was Jesus born in? (Bethlehem)

● Where did they put Jesus after he was born? (In a feeding box)

Put the pieces of construction paper on the floor in a circle, and have a child stand on each one. Say: **To help us remember the story and to work up an appetite for birthday cake, we're going to have a cake walk.**

Have the whole group sing favorite Christmas songs and walk in rhythm around the circle. After the verse, have them stop. Read a question about the Christmas story, and have the group decide who's standing on the correct answer. When they choose the correct answer, have that person drop out of the circle and remove the answer card.

Continue until all questions have been answered. Encourage those who drop out to help find answers by reminding them that they'll get refreshments as soon as the group answers all the questions.

5. Cake Break

(You'll need birthday cake, juice, plates, napkins, forks and cups.)

When all questions are answered, cheer the accomplishment. Sing

"Happy Birthday" to Jesus. Then serve the birthday cake and juice. Play Christmas music in the background.

6. Gifts for Jesus

(The week before, send a letter to parents asking them to help their children buy a small toy for a child in need. Have a few extras for those who don't bring anything. You'll also need a manger or stroller, wrapping paper, tape and scissors.)

Remind children of the toys they brought, and give time for those without toys to choose one from the extras. Then explain that they're each going to give their toys to Jesus as a birthday present. And the church will give them for Jesus to the children in town who wouldn't normally get a Christmas present.

Give children time to wrap their presents, then collect the presents in the manger or stroller. Thank the children for their gifts. Later, deliver the gifts to an appropriate distribution center or shelter in your community.

7. The Gift of Ourselves

(You'll need red and green tempera paint, markers, the banner from activity 2, flat pans for paint, old shirts, newspaper to cover the floor and supplies to clean hands.)

Say: **In addition to the toys we gave to Jesus, we can also give Jesus part of ourselves. For example, we can pray, we can sing praises or we can help others. We're going to show what we can give to Jesus by painting it on the banner we created when we decorated the room.**

Cover kids' good clothes and cover the floor around the banner. Have kids each make hand prints on the banner using the tempera paint in flat pans. Then have them use their fingers to draw something they'll give to God.

After everyone is finished, clean up and ask children to explain what they want to give. Pray, thanking Jesus for the special children who have so much to give to him. Display the banner in your church.

8. Confetti Cheer

(You'll need the confetti made during activity 2.)

To end the lesson, teach children the following rhythmic cheer. When they've learned it, repeat it three times and throw confetti in the air all together the final time. Here's the cheer:

Celebrate! Celebrate!
Jesus has a birthday.
Celebrate! Celebrate!
Christmas is the day! (throw confetti third time through)

by Mike Gillespie

CONTRIBUTORS

Karen M. Ball is an editor in Illinois.

Patti Chromey works with children in her church in Missouri.

Mike Gillespie is a director of Christian education in Kansas.

Cindy S. Hansen, a freelance editor in Colorado, is the former managing editor of Group Books.

Ray and Cindy Peppers live in Georgia, where he is a Christian educator and she is an insurance agent.

Eugene C. Roehlkepartain, a former editor at Group Books, is a director of publication services in Minnesota.

Jolene L. Roehlkepartain, former editor of CHILDREN'S MINISTRY Magazine, is a freelance writer in Minnesota.

Jane P. Wilke is an early childhood educator in Missouri.

Paul Woods is managing editor of Group Books.

PRACTICAL HELP FOR CHILDREN'S MINISTRY...

LIVELY BIBLE LESSONS

You can make creative teaching a snap with these 20 complete children's Bible lessons for each age level. Lively is better, because kids learn more. Each lesson has at least six child-size activities including easy-to-do crafts, action songs, attention-grabbing games and snacks that reinforce the message. Plus, innovative new lessons are included to celebrate holidays like Valentine's Day, Easter, Thanksgiving, and Christmas. Just read the simple instructions, gather a few easy-to-find supplies, and you're ready to go!

Preschoolers
ISBN 1-55945-067-3

Kindergarten
ISBN 1-55945-097-5

Grades 1-2
ISBN 1-55945-098-3

ESTEEM BUILDERS FOR CHILDREN'S MINISTRY

Now Sunday school teachers have an effective new resource to help children from preschool through sixth grade learn to affirm and serve other children and adults. You'll get 101 esteem-building activities, including games, art projects, and service projects that will help children...

- develop their own positive self-image,
- understand how God views them as his creations,
- appreciate the God-given differences between people, and
- learn how to affirm others by their words and actions.

Each activity is easy to prepare; just gather a few easy-to-find supplies, or photocopy one of the handouts included in the book. Makes a great opening exercise as children arrive in class.

ISBN 1-55945-174-2

Order today from your local Christian bookstore, or write: Group Publishing, Box 485, Loveland, CO 80539. For mail orders, please add postage/handling of $4 for orders up to $15, $5 for orders of $15.01+. Colorado residents add 3% sales tax.

MORE CREATIVE RESOURCES FOR YOUR CHILDREN'S MINISTRY...

SNIP-AND-TELL BIBLE STORIES

Karyn Henley

Your children will watch in awe as Bible stories literally unfold before their very eyes. Each Bible story has a photocopiable pattern for you to fold and cut as you tell the story. The figures you create are key parts of the story, such as...

- the snake, the tree, and the fruit from the Garden of Eden (Genesis 3);
- Moses in the basket (Exodus 1—2:10);
- Samson and his hair—which you cut off (Judges 16);
- the lion from Daniel and the lions' den (Daniel 6);
- a string of wise men (Matthew 2:1-12);
- Jairus' daughter sitting up in bed (Mark 5:21-43);
- the fish from when Jesus fed 5,000 people (John 6:1-13);

...and more stories from both the New and Old Testaments!

Photocopiable patterns let you practice cutting and telling the story ahead of time—and patterns are easy to follow. The solid lines show you where to cut, while the dotted lines show you where to fold. And discussion questions about the story allow you to get the children involved—by having younger children help tell the story if they know it—or having older children help cut and fold the patterns.

ISBN 1-55945-192-0

CRAFTS & MORE FOR CHILDREN'S MINISTRY

Karyn Henley & Lois Keffer

Use active learning to get your kids working while they're learning. Each craft activity includes a supply list for quick preparation. The lessons start with an activity using elements of the Bible stories. You then read and discuss the stories with your kids. Crafts to make include...

- toast tablets resembling the Ten Commandments (Exodus 19:9—20:21),
- paper cup chariots to tell the story of Elijah (2 Kings 2:1-18),
- paper wads and human shields to show how the three men were protected in the fiery furnace (Daniel 3),
- the manger scene to learn how God keeps his promises to us (Luke 2:1-7),

...and more! And crafts are ideal for any children's ministry setting, including...

- Sunday school,
- vacation Bible school,
- children's church,
- Wednesday night programs,
- after school clubs,

...or any time kids get together.

ISBN 1-55945-191-2

Order today from your local Christian bookstore, or write: Group Publishing, Box 485, Loveland, CO 80539. For mail orders, please add postage/handling of $4 for orders up to $15, $5 for orders of $15.01+. Colorado residents add 3% sales tax.

FUN, INNOVATIVE RESOURCES FOR CHILDREN'S MINISTRY

FUNTASTIC SKITS FOR CHILDREN'S MINISTRY

Get your kids off their chairs and into the action. Your kids will experience Bible lessons firsthand, while affirming their abilities and talents to act. Skit topics include...

- growing up (Jeremiah 29:11-13),
- trust (Matthew 14:22-33),
- being liked by others (John 15:18-25),
- divorce (Romans 8:31-39),

...and more. Skits on Bible characters include such notables as...

- Lazarus
- Jonah
- Esther

...and others! Follow-up discussion starters get kids involved with the lesson—and talking about key issues in their world. Plus, skits are easy to use and quick to prepare—with no rehearsals necessary. And there are lots of practical ideas on involving kids in the drama, pointers on inspiring kids while keeping control in the classroom, and other helpful planning hints.

ISBN 1-55945-162-9

PUZZLE FUN

These fun and challenging puzzles make great gifts for children. And children's workers and Sunday school teachers can use them to teach important lessons about working together to reach a common goal. The finished puzzles each illustrate an important Bible story and provide visual aids to help children understand the stories better. Puzzles are for ages five and up and have 150 pieces. Plus, each puzzle comes with suggested lesson ideas for children's workers.

The Christmas Story Bible Puzzle
ISBN 1-55945-260-9

The Adventures of Moses Bible Puzzle
ISBN 1-55945-262-5

Order today from your local Christian bookstore, or write: Group Publishing, Box 485, Loveland, CO 80539. For mail orders, please add postage/handling of $4 for orders up to $15, $5 for orders of $15.01+. Colorado residents add 3% sales tax.